D1366286

Confessions of a Secular Jesus Follower

ALSO BY TOM KRATTENMAKER

The Evangelicals You Don't Know

Onward Christian Athletes

Confessions of a SECULAR Jesus Follower

Finding Answers in Jesus
for Those Who Don't Believe

Tom Krattenmaker

CONVERGENT
NEW YORK

Copyright © 2016 by Tom Krattenmaker

All rights reserved.
Published in the United States by Convergent Books,
an imprint of the Crown Publishing Group,
a division of Penguin Random House LLC, New York.
crownpublishing.com
convergentbooks.com

CONVERGENT BOOKS is a registered trademark and its C colophon is a trademark of Penguin Random House LLC.

The primary Bible translation used in this book is the NIV, with the NKJV cited twice, and the KJV, NET, and ESV translations each cited once. In addition, some renderings are paraphrased by the author for ease of reading but not at the expense of the text's intended meaning.

Grateful acknowledgment is made to Alain de Botton for permission to reprint an excerpt from "Easter for Atheists," originally published on ThePhilosophersMail.com.

Library of Congress Cataloging-in-Publication Data is available upon request.

ISBN 978-1-101-90642-2
eBook ISBN 978-1-101-90643-9

Printed in the United States of America

Jacket design by Alane Gianetti

10 9 8 7 6 5 4 3 2 1

First Edition

To my mother, Ceil,
for giving me the gift of determination
and perseverance, without which no books
would ever be written

CONTENTS

Confessions of a Secular Jesus Follower

INTRODUCTION

During my mountain-climbing days, I came to appreciate the value of ropes and, especially, anchors. When the climb team must negotiate a steep, slippery pitch, where falls are both possible and highly damaging to one's prospects for survival, a fixed line is laid. Each climber latches on to that lifesaving rope by means of a sliding knot at the end of a short rope that's attached to his or her harness. That knot slides easily as you push it up with your hand, over and over, while you carefully ascend on the snowy slope or rock face. But that knot can grab and hold the fixed line—that lifeline—like bulldog jaws when subjected to the kind of sudden, downward jerk that happens when a climber starts to fall.

Those Prusik knots work amazingly well if you tie them right. But even then, the fixed rope has to be secured by an anchor that will not suddenly break loose, that will hold firm in the critical moment you hope will never come. A massive, unmovable rock is ideal, one with a shape that makes it impossible for the looped rope to slide up and off. Climb leaders set up anchors very carefully; they go to great lengths to choose a dependable rock. Team members are going to be committing their lives to it, after all. The anchor had damn well better not fail.

It's sort of like that in our everyday lives down here in our cities and towns, I've come to see, if or when we finally get around to choosing an anchor on which we are going to bet our lives, if or when we decide to climb for something higher than narrow self-interest, higher than "Me, Me, Me." The concept is not an easy sell in our do-your-own-thing culture, in the midst of a postmodern zeitgeist that tells us there is no fixed line or immovable anchor, that there is no ultimate truth. Even if that's true—even if everything *is* relative—there is value, I have seen, in going all in on a principle and commitment as if it is the final word.

No exclusivist, I'm not going to claim there is only one trustworthy anchor out there. As we all know, many, many people make God belief their rock, people I respect even though it's a leap I am unable to make myself. I know people who have found a worthy anchor in Judaism or Islam, or in Buddhism or Hinduism or other non-Western religions. As a nonreligious person, I have felt inspired by ethically driven seculars who build their lives around serving their communities and working for a more just and equitable world. I have been moved by a good-hearted atheist testifying to the life-changing value she has derived from treating *Jane Eyre* as her sacred text. All of these I respect, and I am open to the value of many other sources of uplift and inspiration. I do not, however, accept that pretty much anything will suffice as our ultimate anchor and our basis for a life of substance. Buying stuff—which often seems our culture's preferred approach—certainly won't.

On the mountains I've climbed, figuratively speaking, I've discovered, and then rediscovered again and again, the anchor that means the most to me, the anchor I find most worthy of my trust. It's the ethic and the inspiration and, indeed, the way of an ancient figure with whom we are acquainted, but whose relevance to our lives and society might not be so readily apparent, and whose availability to us, if we are secular, might come as a complete surprise.

He's the figure you've seen in photos towering over Rio de Janeiro, or looking out at you with pale blue eyes from the sentimental popular paintings that used to be common in America, or hanging in agony on the crucifixes found in many Catholic churches.

Familiar though he is, you probably haven't seen him in the way we are going to on the pages that follow. Let me explain what I mean, and the context in which I mean it. . . .

We live, for worse and for better, in a secular age. Even the religiously devout, with their acceptance of practical science and their nonreliance on the supernatural to navigate and understand the objective world before them—the cause of the common cold, the sources of lightning and earthquakes, the position of the Earth (and us) in the vast universe—assent to secular terms of engagement in ways their faithful predecessors from centuries and millennia past would scarcely recognize. Whatever our religious persuasion, we have little choice in this matter. Because of the timing of our births and the culture in which we live, we *all* inhabit an age and space that emphasize science, technology, and rational, evidence-based persuasion and decision making, while casting reflexive suspicion upon the supernatural. Here in the Western world, we *all* live in a context where our worldviews and frames of reference are matters of our choice, where religious nonbelief is an option—an increasingly viable one, judging from the demographic data—and where religious belief, in some settings and circles more than others, is hard to muster.

It's not surprising, then, to find growing numbers of people in the United States and other Western cultures who are secular through and through: no god, no church, no community built around religious values and commitments.

In these outward-expanding secular spheres, a real-life experiment unfolds. Where there was once reliance on God belief and the structures that grow out of that, there is now an iterative and earnest collective effort to figure out how to do life "naked," to borrow a term from Richard Neuhaus. In his seminal work *The Naked Public Square*, published in 1986, Neuhaus lamented a public square increasingly shorn of religion. Three decades later, a broader unanswered question hangs over us, posed by the rapidly growing legions who would keep religion separate not only from politics and government but from their *lives*. More and more of us are experiencing the ups and downs and triumphs and devastations of human existence—the births and deaths and all the major milestones in between—with no religion to lean on, with no divinely ordered structure to hold us. We face our mortality and all the other vexing mysteries of life naked.

What happens *now* to society, and us?

Despite shrill warnings about the nihilism to which secular living supposedly must lead, despite the claims that without God people are doomed to living life with no notion of right and wrong and good and bad—why not just kill for sport?—most of us in this wildly diverse collection of nonreligious, nontheistic individuals are managing fine, more or less. We are demonstrating every day that godlessness does not lead to the horrors that alarmist religion promoters warn about. We are, for the most part, people who enjoy our lives. We are, by and large and imperfectly, good citizens who tend to our responsibilities, take care of our kids, love our spouses and parents, and try to make the world a fairer and better place. By doing all this with our eyes open to our mortality and while harboring no sweet notion of heaven to console us, we are disproving that seculars crumble under the vast weight of supposed nothingness. We are proving, as the pithy slogan of the American Humanist Association puts it, that people and life can be "good without a god."

Sorry, Phil Robertson of "Duck Dynasty" fame. The reality is worlds different from the picture you paint of an atheist family being murdered and tortured and having no basis to object because, after all, with no God, they have no standard of right and wrong. Sorry, those who agree with John Kasich, who alleged during his 2015 presidential campaign that our country's migration away from traditional religion is robbing us of our morals and values. The reality on the ground shows us that while morality is, yes, changing, it is still there, and the runaway hedonism with which you associate secularity is not materializing. Sorry, drama kings and queens. The mortality that we perceive and accept does not have us secular people enduring daily, head-in-hands agony.

Judging by the perceptive lyrics of one of our decade's best indie rock bands, the secular response to our impending demise appears to combine nonchalance with a stiff upper lip. If we are not already dead, we are on our way there, Metric notes in "Dreams So Real." So . . .

Shut up and carry on,
the scream becomes a yawn

The truth about our secular lives is more complex, prosaic, and maybe even boring than the doomsayers would have us believe. If there is a problem to be discerned in the growing secularity of our time, this is where it's likely to be found. To use a term from the philosopher Charles Taylor, it's in the "flatness" that we experience as people who perceive and experience no supernatural charge in our world and surroundings. In the words of the philosophers Hubert Dreyfus and Sean Dorrance Kelly, our "technological world," when compared against the divinely infused age of old, can seem "impoverished and dull."

For all that is reassuring and even impressive about the good and useful lives being led by the burgeoning numbers of people who are atheist, agnostic, humanist, or utterly indifferent to religion, one can detect a quiet crisis of sorts. It comes in the form of a vacuum—a vacuum of inspiration and meaning—and in an absence of potent means to climb out of our mundane, self-centric existences to something greater than ourselves. So committed to do-it-yourself constructions of life's purpose, so determined to be the captains of our own lives, we can sometimes squander grand opportunities to learn from, to draw inspiration and instruction from, teachers from the past whose insights are timeless and relevant. Forgoing these sources of insight and encouragement can leave us naked in areas of life where we could really use some clothing—particularly those vulnerable areas where a confused and hyperindividualistic culture invades our psyches and calls to us with a siren song of trivial self-seeking that will ultimately leave us crashed on the rocks if that's all we hear, and heed.

We would be wise to avail ourselves of some time-tested input. I'd like to suggest one especially compelling source.

In the pantheon of philosophers, prophets, teachers, artists, moral exemplars, and sages from the ages, one stands out for me as a particularly promising figure for our time. He is a figure of unusual wisdom and deeply moving strangeness who calls me to reconceive the orientation of my own life and the manner in which I engage my fellow humans. His story compels me to access my often-reluctant generosity and pull myself out of my self-centered worries and obsessions. His example has motivated me to befriend people in all manner of categories that are not my own—Muslims, evangelical Christians, LGBT people, and so on—and sympathetically tell their stories on the op-ed page of the nation's largest newspaper. This figure's inspiration has changed the way I treat the supposed nobodies whom I could easily get away with mistreating. His message and manner, I find, address our culture's maladies and malaises amazingly well, as they do my own.

I do not claim there is only one figure or source from whom we can learn and draw inspiration, whom we can emulate. Gandhi, Martin Luther King Jr., Abraham Lincoln, and others have much to offer, and this is not an either-or exploration we are going on in this book. But one figure stands out.

That figure is Jesus.

Wait, what? *Jesus?* Didn't I just say I am secular? Aren't I a little *confused*?

Well, no. The problem is not any confusion but the lack of a label that describes the path that I have been on for a long time, and that many more might walk if the trailhead were properly marked.

I am, as it turns out, a secular Jesus follower.

I have a thing about Jesus. I have practically always had a fascination with him. From Jesus, I have long drawn inspiration and a deep, albeit fleeting, sense of how to live and how to treat others. In a sense, I grew up around him. From an early age, I have found the approach to life that Jesus espouses on the pages of the Bible infecting my head and heart. I was raised in a Catholic family, attending mass Sunday after Sunday, half-dragged by my dutiful mother. She revealed a great deal about her own level of belief by dropping out of church after her kids had vacated the nest, a dropping-out I would emulate. I always puzzled over and doubted the principal theological propositions about the identity and cosmic role of Jesus, concepts that didn't make sense or ring true to me when I was learning about them in my youth and that still, in my adult years, leave me unmoved. But despite my doubts and despite the boredom I often experienced in the pews, other parts of church—the stories about Jesus, the portrayals of his compassionate humanity in verses and hymns—took up permanent residence in me. I can still hear in my memory, as if being sung right now, the strains of the pretty song with the beautiful idea about how to regard other people, especially those on the bottom rungs. (Forgive the gender-exclusive language, which I am told has been updated in more recent years.)

> *Whatsoever you do to the least of my brothers,*
> *that you do unto me*

But here is the complication: I am, in every significant way, a secular person—*secular* in the colloquial sense of the word, as in "not religious." I belong to no church. When I darken the door of one, it's as an observer, researcher, or someone's invited friend. Follow me around for a few days, and you will notice that I do not use religious language. I am not the type who will promise to pray for you if you are in distress, although I am more than willing to keep you in my thoughts and heart, offer you a shoulder to cry on, and lend a hand if there is something I can do.

I do not believe Jesus died for the forgiveness of my sins, factually speaking, so that I might enjoy eternal life in heaven. Nor do I believe that it is literally and factually true that Jesus was, and is, God—which is not surprising when you realize I am not convinced of the existence of God either. As naturally follows, I am unpersuaded that Jesus literally, factually rose from the dead and that he literally, factually appeared to his disciples in the flesh in the ensuing days, going so far as to have Doubting Thomas (my namesake, fittingly) literally, factually stick his fingers into his pierced flesh.

I do not believe my assent to a discrete set of theological

propositions about Jesus will save me from my anxieties, my flaws, my selfishness, my petty worries, and my ever-approaching expiration date as a human being—although as you will read on the pages ahead, I am vexed by these things and could really use some "saving" from them, a kind of saving that a secularly understood Jesus can quite ably help us experience.

And what of hell? I find its presence all too real in our lives and societies, in the hellish experiences everyone bears—some, alas, much more than others. But that's as far as my credulity will stretch. As for heaven, that, too, is a bridge too far for me. I do believe, however, that glimpses and whiffs of something finer, something bigger than ourselves, can occasionally be ours, and our lives are finer for them. I am not talking about eternal life or other supernatural phenomena. I am talking about experiences of inspiration, of getting outside ourselves and our narrow self-interest, experiences that usually have something to do with beauty and compassion, with acts of selflessness and love.

Jesus, I suggest, can help us access that "something finer." And despite my inability to accept the religious claims about his cosmic status, I believe Jesus is the answer, or at least a large part of it—if only we can work out what question we are asking and the language we are using to address it.

I recall a moment sitting in my father's car as a seventeen-year-old revealing to him that I did not subscribe to the principal doctrines about Jesus espoused by the church to which my dad was so devoted. This did not please him. But I remember, too, in that same conversation, avowing a fascination with Jesus and a devotion to what he stands for. "To me, it doesn't matter if he literally rose from the dead," I recall declaring to my father, aware that my statement was a deal breaker with respect to my qualifying as a Christian. What Jesus said and did is *true* regardless, I tried to explain—true, as in speaking profoundly to the human condition and showing us a different kind of human experience, a different and better world. (I am sure my articulation of the idea was one thousand times clumsier that day in my father's car.)

I hear echoes of that conversation when I think of a memorable e-mail dialogue I had decades later with an evangelical. So, he asked incredulously, I believe Jesus was "just another man"?

"No, I would never say that Jesus was 'just another man,'" I responded. We might as well call him the "son of God," I went on to say, if that is a useful way to signify his unparalleled status and staying power over the two millennia since his life and death, and to elevate the significance of his teachings and example. I was at it again, I realize now—translating the language of Christianity to make it accessible, meaningful, and believable to me.

As I piece together these conversations and others like them, I realize I have been undertaking a decades-long project of sorts. Mine has been an ongoing exertion to clear a space to engage Jesus without being a Christian—a space for me and other interested nonreligious people to do something that society and the religious affiliation categories would apparently forbid us to do: seriously follow Jesus. That is to say, to attempt, as much as it's possible, to act as he did, to treat other people as he did, to understand life as he did.

I continue this quest not in opposition to Christianity, its adherents, and the institutions and structures through which they pursue their faith, but out of massive respect for the religion's central figure, and in the hope that those who cannot or will not sign up for the official religion can draw meaning, hope, and ethical guidance from Jesus.

My quest finds its culmination in this book.

The term *secular Jesus follower* is not exactly in wide circulation. At the time I launched this project, a search of the Internet revealed just one appearance of the exact phrase, and that, in a reader comment beneath an obscure blog post.

Yet I contend that the idea enjoys great and growing, albeit unarticulated, resonance—and that it can address a longing or need felt by many. Consider the ways in which the landscape is shifting in this, our more secular century.

Christianity is losing "market share" in the United States. Add up the percentage of those who identify as religiously unaffiliated and those who are "religious" in name only, belonging to no religious community and participating in no organized religious activity, and you realize that more than 40 percent of this country's large population is unchurched.[1] Where are these people looking for inspiration and ethical guidance? Who or what can they follow?

The search is on. A decade out from Sam Harris's *The End of Faith* and the other bestselling "New Atheism" manifestos of the century's first decade, the leading representatives of nonbelief are spending less time attacking religion and more time pursuing what Americans have traditionally derived from their participation in churches, synagogues, and other religious institutions: community; shared experiences of service, joy, wonder, and compassion; a means to cope with anxiety and loss; a basis for being and doing good;

and a desire to increase happiness and alleviate suffering, in their own lives and the lives of others. How telling that Harris himself, in his 2014 book *Waking Up*, trains his sights not on what's wrong with religion but on the life-enhancing benefits of meditation as part of a wider pursuit of spirituality without religion.

As efforts like Harris's suggest, something subtle, something difficult to pin down, is missing from a life restricted to the material world of me, here, and now. This matters. Sociological research finds that as religion recedes in the affluent Western countries, so does our sense of having clear meaning and purpose in our lives. So does our ability to experience the kinds of close communities in which our emotional needs are often best met. No mere abstractions, these conspicuous absences have real consequences. Most alarmingly, they correlate with higher suicide rates, according to exhaustive research published by the Association for Psychological Science.[2] Ironic indeed: The parts of the world that enjoy the most material comfort have come to be the least religious—and the societies most plagued by a sometimes debilitating poverty of purpose, meaning, and community.

Coupled with this shifting context is the intriguing reality that Jesus, despite decades of culture-war battles over Christianity in politics, remains remarkably unscathed in the public imagination. The religion with which he is associated has endured one PR bruising after another over recent decades; Christianity bashing is oft-heard and easy to find. Jesus, to a remarkable degree, somehow remains above the fray and out of the firing lines. As this suggests, Jesus and Christianity are not one and the same. One can sense a respect for Jesus, even a fascination with him, despite the decline of institutionalized Christianity.

Krista Tippett, host of the acclaimed radio program *On Being* and a recipient of the National Humanities Medal in 2013, notes a "renaissance in the understanding of Jesus." This renaissance, she says, "is not restricted to Christians or to inside the church. . . . I sense that the person of Jesus is very powerful and compelling."[3] Picking up on her point, the author Brian McLaren, whom Tippett was interviewing when she made that comment, offers, "If we say, 'Hey, let's talk about Jesus,' we end up in fascinating discussions very different than 'Let's talk about Christianity.' "

Indeed we do.

Writing about the ways in which Christianity in our time has been "hijacked" by right-wing politics—a common lament among those outside the conservative Christian world—the progressive believer Mark Sandlin exhorts Jesus followers to advance a different conception of Jesus. "When they accuse us of being un-Christian (and they will)," Sandlin writes, "we must stand strong and tell them, 'you no longer get to own that word. . . . We are taking our religion back—way back. All the way back to the teachings of Jesus.' "[4]

I join Sandlin in the quest to return to Jesus and what we can learn from him—but not in quite the same way. It is not my aim to reclaim the Christian religion in the manner suggested by Sandlin. Nor is it my objective in this book to join the scholars who pursue the historical Jesus—the historically and journalistically accurate Jesus—as important as that quest might be. I am interested, rather, in what we might describe as "face-value Jesus," the Jesus who says and does things on the pages of the New Testament. I am not worried for now about the factual accuracy of those accounts or the religious assertions that arise from them. His stories and instruction are valuable and "true," I contend, whether they are journalistically accurate or not.

Yet like Sandlin, I aim to travel "all the way back"—back to a Jesus stripped of theology, doctrine, and present-day political appropriations to the extent that is possible. I will travel back for the sake of jumping to the present and applying Jesus to our lives and times in the twenty-first century, to see what Jesus's example and teachings have to offer us today.

I am convinced they offer a lot. Recent experience is bearing this out for me as I examine and, indeed, change my own life in accordance with what I see and hear from Jesus, and as I examine, in my writing life, the ways in which the Jesus ethic is so often relevant and potentially game-changing for our society. Helping propel these explorations are the secular conversations about Jesus that I've been part of in the discussion group I lead for the Yale Humanist Community—the pithily named "WTF?" as in "Who to Follow?" (More about that in this book's epilogue.)

In the chapters ahead, we will imagine ways in which we can draw inspiration and ethical instruction from Jesus, as individuals and as a society, whatever our religious beliefs. We will consider ways in which the ethic of Jesus can be transformative, whether the affliction is our violence, our anxiety, or our racism, whether the issue is dehumanizing aspects of sex culture or our tendency to demonize "the other," whether the problem is our habit of turning away from those who suffer or our insistence on looking for fulfillment in all the wrong places.

In the end, I hope you will see the ways in which this adds up to a surprising conclusion about Jesus: that his way can be helpful and, indeed, available to non-Christians, and that no one can stop us seculars from following this ethical leader even if we do not or cannot believe the religious aspects of the story. This is a following we could commit to, I argue, not because Jesus is the divine son of God but because the content of his teaching is of such unusually high and enduring quality.

The stakes are high. The conversation is well worth having. Because what, in the final analysis, could be more worthy of our considerations and conversations than the kinds of lives we are going to lead, individually and collectively?

Whether you are atheist, agnostic, or just plain indifferent to religion, whether you are Muslim or Buddhist or Jewish or part of another religion, or whether you're a Christian with a curiosity about how your Jesus appears to someone outside your religion, I hope you will find this volume helpful—even inspirational.

I am glad to have you with me for the journey.

Chapter One

BAD COMPANY

It was not *their* mosque that had just been firebombed in an act of malicious retribution. It was not *their* people who were under threat following the sensationalized news about the young Muslim man caught scheming to bomb a Christmas tree-lighting ceremony up the road in Portland. It was not *their* religion being vilified as a menace to civilization. Yet there they were, a few hundred non-Muslim people from in and around Corvallis, Oregon, circling the Islamic center, where the acrid smell of smoke still hung. Relighting their candles over and over in defiance of the wind and rain, they kept vigil. This was to dissuade any hate-filled arsonist who might be bent on finishing the job. It was also to make a point: The embattled Muslim minority in their community, reviled by many in a culture still traumatized by the 9/11 terrorist attacks and the wars that followed—a war between *their* religion and *ours,* as many Americans saw it—would not be wrongly blamed, would not face this alone.

The community members in the newly formed "Not in Our Town" coalition, together with the local Muslims who worshiped at the mosque, were making a statement by coming together. So said a man named Mohammed Siala, who was the director of the Islamic center, where the bomb-plot suspect had sometimes worshiped during his time as a student at nearby Oregon State University.

"We are sending a clear message to the whole world," Siala declared at the vigil, "to learn from this small city and the big people here. The lesson they should know is that people of different races, genders, and nationalities are here side by side . . . supporting each other and caring for each other and loving each other.

"If we can do it here in this small city, then we can do it anywhere in the world."

Yes, we can, difficult though it is. For a clue as to how, realize that the people who organized the circle of protection around the Corvallis mosque, and many of those who stood with their candles in the rain, came from the area's churches. They were, in other words, people whose ethics and behavior (at least in theory) were guided by Jesus. It's true that you don't need to be religious to stand up for people outside your group when they are under siege and unfairly maligned. But just the same, let the display of the church people in Corvallis shine as an uplifting demonstration of the Jesus way—of the Jesus way that pushes against the prevailing winds of our culture and instinct and demonstrates that we human beings can be driven not only by our hate and fear but by our heads and hearts.

Suspicion. Fear. Determination to choose sides based on religion, skin color, gender, sexual orientation, political allegiances. The urge to pin a large scarlet *E* on the others, on our "enemies." We seethe with these impulses, many of us. We sort ourselves into rival camps and fiercely compete to "take back" our country, as if it were once ours before "they"—they with their suspect way of life and dastardly deeds—somehow stole it from us. We nurse our grievances. We see only the worst in those on the other side, the *wrong* side, and only the best in ours.

As a secular progressive, I have felt the sting of the scapegoating. People like me are the downfall of society, some say. We have no morals. We don't love our country. We disrespect the institutions that make America great—the military, the church, the family. Some prominent religious conservatives go so far as to blame 9/11 and other calamities on the liberals, whose support for the legal availability of abortion and tolerance for homosexuality brings down the wrath of God, as the story goes.

Reeling from this onslaught of blame, from these portrayals of me and "my people" that are distorted beyond all recognition, I sometimes find myself wanting to stand up, grab a megaphone, and shout back: *Hey, you know nothing about us. You have no idea about how we live and what we're like!*

Yet in more generous moments I must ask: How much do I really know about *them*?

Under the influence of my mentor professor in my graduate program at Penn (the one who got me to see my capacity for bigoted portrayals of my "others"), under the influence of the editor I worked with at *USA Today* (who called me out when I indulged my own blame-game tendencies)—under the influence of a Jesus who refused to limit his contact to those on the "acceptable people" list of his place and time—I catch myself sometimes now. A pesky thought worm in my head challenges me with questions I am otherwise reluctant to consider:

Am *I* able and willing to see the humanity in those who are not like me?

Am *I* getting to know people who look and think and believe and vote the "wrong" way?

Hanging Out with the Wrong People

I am hardly the first to say this about Jesus, but it bears repeating: Jesus hung out with the wrong people. Actually, it's worse than that. He ate meals, engaging in acts of intimate community, with people who were anathema to the pious of his day.

Jesus touched the untouchable. Literally.

For instance:

As the Gospel of Matthew tells it, Jesus had just come off the mountain where he had laid down the powerful teachings that came to be known as the Sermon on the Mount. He had just dispensed a body of material that would become part of the wisdom of the ages, schooling his listeners in the hills to be merciful, to be humble, to be peacemakers. Teaching is one thing; doing is another. Would Jesus practice what he preached?

Readers of Matthew don't have to wait long to find out. For within twenty words we read that a leper, of all people, emerges from the crowd walking with Jesus after his sermon. The leper gets Jesus's attention. He has something big to ask: Will Jesus make him clean?

The gospel writer could not be accused of subtlety here.

This was not merely a poor man, a dirty man, an ugly man, a pagan man, or a disreputable man who was seeking to interact with Jesus. This was a leper, part of a group so off-limits as to be quarantined in distant removes where no one would have to look at them, much less touch them. Some religious teachers justified this cruelty by not only making the practical point about leprosy being contagious but portraying these sad souls as subjects of divine punishment. If there was anyone you didn't want to engage with, it was a leper.

The leper beseeches Jesus: "If you are willing, you can make me clean."

Jesus obliges, and then some. Whereas in some Jesus-healing stories the healing is transmitted from afar, this one features direct physical contact. Jesus *touches* the leper. "I am willing," he says. "Be clean."

And clean the man was. Take the healing as a miracle. Or take it as metaphor. Touching the despised other, literally or figuratively, whether by handshake or conversation, whether by extending friendship or learning what it's like to walk in that person's shoes, can have a profoundly positive effect on that person and the wider world. And on you.

Who are our "untouchables"? Who do we treat as the wrong types of people? If you're like many Americans, Muslims might be at the top of the list. There is a tendency among some in our culture to paint all Muslims, including the vast, vast majority, who are peaceful and reject the religious legitimacy of terrorism—who are horrified by what is done in the name of their cherished religion—with the same brush we use to condemn the evil deeds of violent extremists. The tendency is typified by this remark from the prominent United States Senator Lindsey Graham, made while he was running for president in 2015: "Everything that starts with 'Al' in the Middle East," Graham declared, "is bad news." (*Al* basically means "the" in Arabic, and in addition to appearing in the names of terrorist groups like Al Qaeda, it happens to be part of the name of everything from pro soccer teams to universities to humanitarian NGOs in that region of the world.) Graham's point: Everything Islamic in the Middle East is bad. Of course, Graham's claim seems pale next to the proposal made by his then-rival Donald Trump a few months later, Trump declaring that all Muslims should be barred from entering the United States. Reflective of this same ugly tide, anti-Muslim hate crimes in the United States have increased fivefold since the 9/11 attacks.[1]

Sad to say, Muslims have company on the list of groups that are targets for malicious bigotry in our country. LGBT people, atheists, African Americans and other ethnic minorities—these groups and others, too, have borne the weight of prejudice and blame. So have Christians, frankly, depending on the context—a matter we will explore shortly.

Here is how this lamentable human tendency manifested in the spring of 2015—and how a Jesus sighting of sorts brought the episode to a heartening close.

Members of an Arizona motorcycle gang, brandishing guns and insults, staged an anti-Islam rally outside a mosque in their community, complete with a "draw Muhammad" cartoon contest. It was, at its core, a blatant attempt to taunt, menace, and provoke a small, unpopular, and powerless minority. Fortunately, the mosque attendees resisted any urge to mount their own retaliatory threat of violence. Had they not, who knows what kind of killing might have ensued?

It's depressing but true that some of the anti-Islam

protesters implicated Christianity in the debacle, shouting: "Islam is evil, Christ is King." I think it's clear they were engaging their "Christianity" as a tribal identity, not as a Jesus-shaped way of life.

A far better representation of Jesus *did* happen a few days later, however, when a collection of faith groups—Jews and Christians, together with Muslims—staged their own rally at the embattled mosque to show support for the people who worshiped there. Attendees brought flowers and placed them on the windowsills of the building as a sign of peace and solidarity. They called the rally "Love Is Stronger Than Hate."

The world would be more like that if we were to truly follow Jesus.

Get to Know People Before You Hate Them

A newcomer to Portland in 2007, I was looking for an area Muslim leader to interview for a column-in-progress on the wrongs of Muslim bashing, examples of which were flashing in the news with alarming regularity. Why was it my problem? Call it my knee-jerk liberalism, my wanting to stick up for underdogs and those subject to discrimination. Call it my disgust with faulty logic and broad-brush condemnations. Call it my Jesus motivation. Whatever the source, I was appalled and needed to speak out.

When Wajdi Said, head of the locally based Muslim Educational Trust, met me for lunch and conversation at the college where I worked, I mangled things a bit. Because of my inexperience being around Muslims, I subjected my friendly guest to some not-well-informed questions and occasional awkwardness—"highlighted" by my stupidity as I walked him through the cafeteria and explained the culinary lay of the land. Yes, a pork dish was on offer, and yes, before my head could catch up with my mouth, I suggested to my Muslim guest that it might be a tasty option for him. My cheeks burned the moment the words left my lips. *Idiot,* I said to myself. *Muslims don't eat pork. Good job insulting your guest, Tom!* If Wajdi was annoyed, as he had every right to be, he did not let on.

Wajdi educated me that day, and on many other days in the ensuing years, about the experience of being a Muslim in post-9/11 America. A big part of it was always having to brace for the backlash when headlines hit with news about violence committed by Muslim terrorists. As I came to see, Wajdi, like nearly all Muslims, was saddened and horrified by the violence. He was quick to condemn it and adept at refuting it through appeals to the Koran and Muslim tradition. Wajdi was not interested in battling with people of different beliefs and ethnic identities. What did interest him was educating and serving the community (the wider community, not just Muslims) and building bridges between people of different religions. What he did care about was his family—those in the area and those still in Yemen—and his friends.

As I came to learn, those friends were legion. Wajdi's friends included Catholics, Protestants, Jews, Muslims, and others. Many of them had come together after 9/11 to do what they could to make sure our country did not punish innocent Muslim Americans the way we had punished innocent Japanese Americans sixty years earlier, in the aftermath of the Pearl Harbor attack.

This circle drew me in, too. I became a friend to Wajdi, and a friend to many of the seemingly innumerable people who were likewise his friends. I accepted, on multiple occasions, his invitations to visit the school and community center run by his organization, to meet the teachers and kids. I attended his community's Saturday night potluck dinners, which filled up a large community center at a local university. I accepted his invitations to be the featured speaker at one of those gatherings and to serve as moderator at several panel events hosted by his organization, exploring issues like Islam and violence, gender roles in Islam, and how to combat Islamophobia. One night, I was deeply pleased to accept a plaque and public appreciation at a large gathering of the Portland-area Muslim community. I was dubbed, officially, "Friend of the Muslim Educational Trust."

Given the cultural context—given my understanding of Jesus and his insistence on associating with the "others" of his time and place—I can think of no label I would wear more proudly: friend of Muslims.

The senders of the hate e-mail, and those who posted outraged reader comments, saw it quite another way after I wrote a column expressing sympathy and concern for my Muslim friends following the bombing plot mentioned at the opening of this chapter. A dozen or so people tracked down my e-mail address to inform me in six different ways that supporting the Muslims in my community made me an idiot and, worse, a lender of comfort to the enemy—"a complete fool, a silly ass, a dolt," as one charmingly put it. (He apologized when I replied—it was mid-December, after all—with a quick note asking, "Not even a 'Merry Christmas'?")

"Get to Know a Muslim Rather Than Hate One." This

was the headline of a *USA Today* column I wrote on a different occasion decrying the demonization of Muslims. Sounds sensible, doesn't it? Look before you leap, learn before you hate. There is more than common sense and decency driving that sentiment. Sociological research shows a correlation between Americans' opinions about a group other than their own—favorable or unfavorable?—and the number of people in that group with whom they have friendly contact.[2] This helps explain why acceptance of LGBT people has advanced so rapidly over our lifetimes: More and more gay people came out, and more and more of the rest of us experienced their company, learning that they bore no resemblance to the picture of depravity conjured by those opposing them.

Roughly two-thirds of Americans say in surveys they don't know a Muslim. "What they know is ISIS, al Qaida, and Charlie Hebdo," says Todd Green, a religion professor who studies Islamophobia.[3] What they know about Muslims is, in other words, almost nothing.

There are data, logic, and common decency compelling us to get to know the Muslims and other "others" in our community. And then there's Jesus—the Jesus who incurred the wrath of the authorities in his own community by honoring the humanity of those he was supposed to dehumanize, and taking it one infuriating step further by actually being with them.

WWJH? Who would Jesus hate?

Crossed Off Jesus's List

"Jesus said 'hello' much more often than he said 'good-bye.'"

So writes a Christian blogger named Kurt Willems. He's right. For example, when Jesus relates the Parable of the Good Samaritan—a story in which a member of an outcast group, the Samaritans, emerges as the moral exemplar—he does so right after Jesus and his crew experience rejection by a Samaritan village. A couple of the disciples, understandably upset by the Samaritans' cold shoulders, grouse angrily about summoning "fire from heaven" to "consume them" in retaliation.

Jesus, of course, rebukes the disciples for this kind of reaction as it's reported in the Gospel of Luke. And then he proceeds in virtually the next breath to make a Samaritan an ethical hero for the ages. *That* is generosity. *That* is crazy.

You might know the parable. A crime victim is lying at the side of the road, badly injured. Two high-status religious authorities walk by, ignoring the man's plight. The third man to pass is the Samaritan; *he* is the one who comes to the aid of the injured man. The story stops you in your tracks not just because of what the Samaritan does but because of who he is, because of the low, outcast status he bears in the eyes of the pious religious society of which Jesus was a part. Because of their supposedly wrong beliefs and way of life, Samaritans were anathema to the religiously correct people who were Jesus's community, and to whom Jesus was telling this story.

Why would Jesus tell his story so that the wrong thing

was done by the supposedly good guys—the respectable men of status who belonged to Jesus's religious tribe—and the right thing was done by the "bad" guy?

There is something important to learn from this. It challenges us when we map it onto our lives and society today. What do we do with the very real possibility that our own kind sometimes does the wrong thing, and the "other" kind sometimes does what's right? Who do we write off, who do we dehumanize—who do we judge all bad and capable of doing only bad—on the basis of skin color, immigration status, religion, or political affiliation?

Depending on our allegiances and identities, the Samaritan for us may be a young African American man in a hoodie, a Muslim woman wearing a burka, a redneck, a lesbian, a Southern Baptist, a transgendered person. The Samaritan for us may be a flaming liberal or a Tea Party Republican. I am someone's Samaritan. So are you.

As I think hard about Jesus's words and deeds on the pages of the New Testament, as I reflect on the uplifting deeds I have seen committed by some of those who claim him as their savior, as I contemplate why he is such an inspiration to me, this is what shines. This is what makes Jesus such a question, and solution, to our culture today. Left to our instincts, we want to stick with our own kind and stick it *to* the other, all the while basking in reassurances that ours is the right way. The way of Jesus won't let us take this obvious and tempting path. The way of Jesus steers us to the wrong side of the tracks and the human beings living over there.

If Jesus had a "shit list," you wouldn't find people on it. You'd find attitudes and actions. Not wrong *people* but wrong ideas, behaviors, and ways of being in the world. He could see the humanity even in the dreaded tax collectors, who were enforcing the severe policies that kept many of Jesus's people in poverty. He could see the humanity even in the soldiers who were carrying out his execution.

In an article titled "Why You Need More Muslim Friends," Jon Huckins, cofounding director of a group called the Global Immersion Project, reminds his fellow Christians that it's the antithesis of Jesus "to only be in relationship with those who are like 'us,' while excluding 'them.'" Huckins goes on to note, accurately: "As we begin to build relationships with those outside of our tradition, we break out of our little bubbles and are able to truly love like Jesus. Jesus never ran in fear from those who were different from him. No, he ran to people who were different."

How refreshing and countercultural—how evocative of Jesus—that when a string of predominantly black Christian churches were burned in the spring and summer of 2015, a group of Muslims rallied to raise more than $100,000 to help those communities recover. If that weren't enough, Muslims teamed up again several months later to raise nearly $200,000 for families of the victims of a mass shooting (perpetrated by a radicalized Muslim couple) at a social services center in San Bernardino, California.

Who are *we* running to, and from?

Two-Timer

Liberals like to see ourselves as defenders of the underdogs, as champions of the mistreated and misunderstood, as advocates for embattled minorities. Wasn't it only natural that

I would use the power of my pen to stand up for religious minorities and the gay community?

If only I had stopped there.

My dealings with, and support for, one group in particular has gotten me in trouble with my fellow secular progressives. For they're the group most toxic of all in the eyes of many of my own kind:

The dreaded evangelical Christians.

As I mentioned earlier, the list of despised "others" in our culture is appallingly long. Depending on the context, Christians are on it, too—especially that more vocal and theologically conservative bunch we know as "evangelicals." It might sound odd to say it, given that a still-strong majority of Americans identify as Christian, but stereotyping and majority-minority statuses depend on context, and in the contexts that have generally been my home base—progressive, post-Christian, postmodern—think *Portlandia*, the TV show—Christians are a distinct minority, especially the more conservative ones. In those contexts, *they* are often the blame magnets. *They* are often the ones bearing the negative stereotypes. *They* are the "others." Why would I want anything to do with *them*?

Jesus made me do it. With the help of some friends.

Before I started getting to know the "fundies," as some in my circle like to call them, my thoughts about them were analogous to what many Americans think they know about Muslims. What I "knew" came from media caricatures and misinformed conversations portraying evangelicals at their worst: the picture of Bible-thumping right-wingers out to malign heathens and religious softies like Unitarians and mainliners, painting them, along with the Muslims and the liberals and the feminists and "the gays," as the downfall of God's favorite nation. As I came out of the gates as a new commentator on religion in public life, I enjoyed shooting off the too-easy criticisms against these people: the hypocrisy, the faulty thinking, the selective morality, the hateful rhetoric.

"Antievangelical bias." This is what I found scribbled in the margin of one of my research papers. The professor who'd become my adviser and mentor in my graduate program at the University of Pennsylvania certainly got my attention with *that*. I fumed for days.

To get my professor off my back, I began to take greater care to at least feign some nuance in what I was writing and saying about evangelicals. No great concession.

As time went on, though, I started meeting some real-life evangelicals. Instigating the process was a filmmaker named Dan Merchant. He had seen a *USA Today* piece I'd written decrying evangelicals' misuse of God in politics, and he wanted to interview me on-camera for his film in progress—a film I assumed had the kind of antievangelical cast I so greatly favored. He told me the title was "Lord Save Us from Your Followers." What was not to like? How surprising to discover after the interview that this hip, hilarious, irreverent, and rock music–loving filmmaker was an evangelical himself—and that he shared many of my concerns and critiques about what conservative Christians were saying and doing in the culture wars that were peaking at the time.

Merchant introduced me to other evangelicals who were breaking stereotypes in and around our city. There was Tony "the Beat Poet" Kriz, known to many as the crazy Christian who hatched the idea of a reverse confession booth at ultrasecular Reed College—the confession booth in which the Christians confessed to the heathen Reedies. There was Kevin Palau, the son of a famed international evangelist and an inveterate relationship builder who was innovating new forms of Christian outreach based on service to the disadvantaged. There was Paul Louis Metzger, a theology professor at evangelical Multnomah Biblical Seminary whose conservative theology was paired with a progressive openness to friendship and mutual learning with people of different ethnicities and religious beliefs.

I met these people for lunch and coffee. I attended their events. I cited their ideas, told their stories, and hailed their stereotype-busting, friend-making ways on the pages of *USA Today.* I spoke a few times at their events and classes. I even found myself a time or two speaking at—gasp—evangelical churches.

I was surprised to discover how much we had in common. But more than that, I was enriched to learn, in the areas where we disagreed, why they saw the world as they did.

Me? A friend of the evangelicals?

Transgress the Boundaries

Engaging with our "others" with a Jesus motivation can lead to all sorts of surprising turns. I am moved by the memorable words of the theology professor and prize-winning author Willie Jennings to describe the enlivening places Jesus will take us if we follow his lead—places that are "transgressive" by the business-as-usual thinking of our divided society and the values that prevail in our market-driven culture. Jennings's words evoke not just community but something one step higher: commun*ion*, the spirit of caring intimacy. This is the kind of "transgression" for which Jesus is notorious—the kind our divided society could really use.

In his book *The Christian Imagination*, Jennings writes:

> The identities being formed in the space of communion may become a direct challenge to the geographic patterns forced upon peoples by the capitalistic logic of real estate. We who live in the new space of joining may need to transgress the boundaries of real estate, by buying where we should not and living where we must not, by living together where we supposedly cannot, and being identified with those whom we should not.[4]

Count me in with the boundary transgressors. I have found that treating our "others" like human beings can lead to experiences that are fascinating, even fun. It can fill you with the surprising satisfaction that comes from doing something out of the ordinary that is thoroughly principled. The bad news: It can make you unpopular in some quarters—your *own* quarters. Breaking out of the tight us-versus-them formations will sometimes bring a slap of disapproval from those who prefer to keep the battle lines straight and the troops on high alert. They will say you are a traitor. They will accuse you of being part of the oh-so-lame "mushy middle."

"I hate goddamn centrists." This is the blunt assertion of the progressive pundit Charles P. Pierce. "There are three kinds of people who claim to be centrists in this country today," Pierce writes. "There are embarrassed Republicans. There are lazy people. And there are liars."[5]

He could not be accused of mincing his words. Or of demonstrating much of an open mind about those who do not share his (and my) true-blue progressivism.

Yes, the middle *can* suck—if it's the middle of cop-outs, convenience, and no convictions. To be generous with Pierce, perhaps this is what he has in mind when he condemns centrists. But there's another middle, the kind of middle where you go with your convictions firing on all cylinders but your mind and heart open to the alleged enemies who meet you there—where you go not in spite of your convictions but *because* of them. Perhaps I romanticize it too much. But I like to think of this as the "radical" middle. And I like to think it's where the transgressive prophet Jesus leads us.

This is the middle where you'll want to have eyes in the back of your head. Because you face fire from both sides as you dart out there, including fire from behind—from your *own* camp.

I experienced this after writing about my interactions with Focus on the Family and complimenting the organization for singing a new tune about gay people. Yes, Focus on the Family—a group seen by people on my side of the tracks as a menace to equal rights for women, sexual minorities, the nonreligious, and liberals in general. By the time I intersected with the people there, Focus was no longer under the leadership of the notorious James Dobson. It was greatly moderating its rhetoric about, and improving its relationship with, members of the gay community. This I hailed in my writing. Some of my progressive readers bought it. Some did not. The reason some called "foul" was that Focus on the Family, despite the new tone and emphasis, despite the bridges it was building to the gay community, still had not endorsed marriage equality for gay and lesbian people.

"Naïve and sugar-coated optimism"—this was the criticism of my work by one unconvinced reader. I had fallen, this critic wrote, for the deceptive "charm campaign" of evangelicals who wanted to improve their image while holding to their noxious political views and opposition to gay marriage. I heard from others—passionate advocates for gay rights, gay people who had experienced the personal pain of demonization—that I had sold them out by publishing a positive word about Focus on the Family. I can understand this reaction. It's not *my* rights and humanity being impinged upon. Indeed, it is easy for *me*—a straight guy—to cut slack for evangelicals who might be evolving on gay rights but who are not (yet) at the point where they will concede to gay couples the dignity and status that go with being married in the eyes of the law.

So it goes when you step out of formation. In this instance, and others like it, what is there to do but acknowledge the pain and understandable distrust that lead some to say "no" to shaking hands in no-man's land? I'll accept the criticism; I'll take the hit. Frankly, it is nothing next to the hits absorbed by my gay fellow citizens. Or Jesus.

No One Is Lost

Remember that firebombed mosque in Corvallis? At the candlelight vigil a few days later, its director declared that whoever set the fire was forgiven—actually forgiven—by him and the others who worshiped at the mosque. Not that they were endorsing bigotry and violence. As Mohammed Siala told the vigil keepers, "We forgive him or them. . . . [But] with your support here tonight, we tell them that there is no place for prejudice toward anybody, regardless of faith or race or nationality."

No, there is no place for hate. But by forgiving them, the mosque administrator essentially said to the perpetrators, "There is a place for *you*." Siala seems to realize that no one is entirely lost. Perhaps he knows of the real-life instances in which even the worst haters, people like neo-Nazi white supremacists, have undergone a radical change of heart and have become champions of tolerance and diversity.

The forgiveness granted by Siala was certainly not earned by those who received it. It was gifted. I have seen other impressive giving of this sort, giving that goes across boundaries and way past our groups' and our own agendas.

I have seen it in the way that the Muslim Educational Trust in my former home city serves and supports not just the city's Muslim minority—which would be entirely understandable—but the whole community.

I have seen it in the way Chris Stedman, a young humanist leader in the Yale community who is both atheist and gay and has faced the wrath of (some) Christians on both counts, continues to model interreligious dialogue and teamwork with Christian organizations and people.

I have seen it in the way an evangelical pastor and theologian named Matthew Croasmun has supported the humanist community that I've joined in my new city of New Haven, attending our events, elevating our ideas, and treating us not as a threat, which some in his shoes might do, but as a friend.

I have seen it in the surprising way in which the president of Southeastern Baptist Theological Seminary, Danny Akin, made a video for the Openly Secular campaign insisting that atheists and other religious "nones" be treated with kindness and respect.

I have seen it in the way that Jesus, in the many stories about him that have lived on, repeatedly and stubbornly refused to shun the people who, by custom and by human instinct, he was supposed to write off.

Call it my naïve idealism. Call it my foolish wish to live in a world in which I don't have to dispense or receive dehumanizing treatment. But I live in hope that this could one day be the norm, not the exception.

So count me in with the boundary crossers who know that acts of bigotry and exclusion against one segment of the community constitute hits on the whole community. Count me in with the idealists who go high road when culture and circumstance tempt them to go low.

And count me in, please, with the Jesus with whom I am not supposed to associate given his location inside a Christendom that is not my world, but whose wisdom and way are far too compelling to be separated from me by anyone's boundary.

Chapter Two

KILLER INSTINCT

Live by the sword, die by the sword.

—Jesus

A violence festers in the heart of humanity, it seems. Or as Bruce Springsteen phrased it in the dark classic "Nebraska" (a song whose narrator is facing execution and answering why he went on his murderous rampage), "I guess there's just a meanness in this world."

This meanness showed itself eleven days before Christmas in 2012, twenty-six miles north and west of where my wife and I live now. After killing his mother with shots to the head, a twenty-year-old named Adam Lanza made the short drive from his home to Sandy Hook Elementary School and proceeded to fatally shoot twenty children and six adult staff members before turning the gun on himself.

Imagine the horror and grief of those whose children, spouses, and parents were murdered that day. As one area pastor described the scene at the firehouse where grieving parents gathered, "They were sobbing, yelling and throwing themselves on the floor."

It's hardly the first time we have reeled from a mass shooting in this country. We remember Columbine, Virginia Tech, the movie theater in Aurora, Colorado, and the social services center in San Bernardino, California. We remember the recent mass bloodletting that came with a strong race-hate theme: Charleston. We remember Orlando.

Mass shootings may not be everyday occurrences. But deadly violence certainly is. People use guns to kill and injure tens of thousands of their fellow human beings each year in this country. It's like a mass shooting spread out over time and space, unfolding in a cultural context that finds us buying, selling, and glorifying violence in the shows and movies we watch and the video games we play. It unfolds in the context of human beings locked in conflict, arguing, burning with anger, lusting after what others possess, wanting to get their adversaries out of their way. It unfolds, too, on a foundation of low-grade, everyday, small-ball "violence"—the kind we nurse in our hearts when we hold on to animosities and grudges against others.

Yes, there is a violence in our hearts—and in our economy, too. In the state where Adam Lanza did his killing, gun manufacturing was once the backbone of the economy. Whitney, Smith & Wesson, Winchester—names you have heard, of men who made fortunes improving firearms technology, producing ever-more-efficient killing machines, and selling them to the military and the public. Once, while listening to a radio news story about tighter gun-control laws being proposed in Connecticut, pre–Sandy Hook, I heard opponents of the law argue that stricter gun regulations would harm the state's economy and job opportunities.

Liberal me, I thought: *So we need to keep the killing going for the sake of a better economy?*

I don't want to sound too naïve. I acknowledge history. Given that the Civil War *was* happening back in the 1860s, and given that the perpetuation or abolition of slavery was at stake in the bloody affair, I am glad that the Spencer repeating rifle, developed in Connecticut, gave Union soldiers an important advantage at the Battle of Gettysburg. But how I wish it hadn't come to that.

Where, you might ask, is Jesus in the midst of all this violence? The Prince of Peace, the religious teacher who, when the guards came to arrest him, admonished a member of his entourage to put away his sword, the serene figure who preached the virtue of peacemaking, the modeler of nonviolence who did nothing to fight his sentencing and execution—where is he in the midst of all this violence in what is often portrayed as a Christian nation?

Where was Jesus when Sandy Hook happened?

If Jesus had been there, would he have been carrying his own gun and would he have eliminated the shooter before all those kids got killed? If Jesus had been there, would he have taken a bullet for someone else? If Jesus had been there, would he have performed a miracle to jam Adam Lanza's gun—or maybe bring the murdered pupils, teachers, and staff people back to life?

The questions are, of course, absurd. Who the hell knows? All is wild speculation. This much is clear, however: There *was* no Jesus in the killing that happened that day, or in the sick dynamics that led to Sandy Hook and the other eruptions of violence we have suffered.

If our country and world were truly infused with the

ethic and example of Jesus, there *would be* no killing sprees and no endless debates about whether we need more or less gun control to prevent them. If we all followed Jesus, we wouldn't have guns and weapons everywhere. This wouldn't be because Jesus, or the laws, had banned them. It would be because our hearts and attitudes and world had changed in such a way, and to such a profound degree, that we would not want them.

The Heart of Violence

The seed of violence is planted deep in human history as well as human hearts. The truth of this was reinforced by a gruesome discovery made by archaeologists working in Germany in 2015. They found the site of a massacre that occurred seven thousand years ago, complete with evidence of torture and mutilation. The perpetrators were clearly capable of "very violent behavior," one of the researchers observed—which made them, he added, "not very different from us."[1]

Our seemingly innocuous references to violence today reveal something about its tenacious presence in the fabric of our culture. The "killer instinct"—this is something we sports fans want our teams to possess. This is the stuff of our competitive nature in business, in career advancement, in politics as well (an issue we will explore in Chapter Nine). When we have the other team on the ropes (that's a boxing idiom, of course, for the moment in a fight when a boxer is one hard punch away from being rendered unable to stand), we want *our* team to put the game away, seal the deal, finish them off. Of course this is relatively harmless (although not to the careers of players too often on the losing end). Of course competition would not work if we felt bad for our opponents and gave them free points to help them "get back in the game." But still . . . we become inured to the consequences borne by our opponents as we, as our side, ruthlessly pursue our goal.

Non-gun-packing citizens are also capable of the hate and anger that nurtures violence. I first noticed the flush of irrational hate in myself when I was a kid in elementary school, finding another boy annoying for the way he talked or looked, and wanting to punch him. I noticed it while playing sports against kids from other parts of our town whom I didn't know. A few kids saw *me* this way. I had a tormentor in eighth grade who let me know what it felt like to be on the receiving end of the hate that burns for no apparent reason.

Despite the arguments we hear that violence is inevitable or necessary, that violence can be redemptive, that violence is often justifiable—that *violence works*—a glimpse into the heart of violence helps us comprehend why, as a method of achieving the peace and stability we purportedly desire, it is ultimately futile. "We can't bomb our way to peace," as one memorable op-ed piece headline put it following the United States' withdrawal from Iraq.[2] In almost every instance, our experience shows that the violence we use to achieve the desired *end* of violence (at least its dramatic reduction) seeds future rounds of violence. Violence, even if it quells an existential threat in a given situation, even if it keeps the enemy at bay for the moment and thwarts the intruder at our door, cannot kill the violence in our hearts. The violence, even if it recedes for a moment, always storms back.

Jesus, if we have the courage to take him seriously, can stop the violence.

Some scholars who trace the history of ethics see Jesus as a figure who brought a whole new paradigm. Rather than focusing solely on human actions, and the rules and laws that attempt to shape and constrain those actions, Jesus directed attention to the source of these actions: the human heart. Note the way he spoke about these matters:

In Matthew 5 (the Sermon on the Mount): "You have heard that it was said . . . 'You shall not commit adultery and anyone who murders will be subject to judgment.' But I tell you that anyone who is angry with a brother or sister will be subject to judgment."

In Mark 7: "It is from within, out of a *person's heart* (emphasis mine), that evil thoughts come."

And, again, in Matthew 5, speaking directly to violence now: "You have heard it said . . . 'You shall not murder, and whoever murders will be in danger of the judgment.' But I say to you that whoever is angry with his brother without a cause shall be in danger of the judgment."

This is actually somewhat irritating if you're a guy like me, who is, for the most part, nonviolent and wants to feel boastful about it. I don't own a gun. I punched a kid only once in my whole childhood. I have the personality type that leads me to defuse potentially hostile situations rather than escalate them. And I want to feel a little superior on this score. Damn it—why does Jesus have to go and spoil my sanctimonious fun?

The Endless Cycle

In the Gaza Strip, the Israeli army had just destroyed the tunnels that Hamas had been using to smuggle in the stuff they couldn't get past the blockades on the ground: food, consumer goods, and, yes, weapons and fighters. This was in the summer of 2014, when the Israelis were taking determined military action to quell the violence rising up from the Palestinian fighters. If you look back at the news reports from the time, you will find Israeli spokespeople sounding quite confident they had succeeded in finding and destroying the dozens of tunnels that laced the subterranean environment just under Gaza.

But look at the news reports just a few months later, and this is what you find: Hamas vowing to rebuild the tunnels. Hamas *succeeding* in rebuilding the tunnels. Hamas *building more tunnels than ever.*

As the Israelis were learning, you can destroy the tunnels but you cannot destroy the impulse in people's hearts that drove them to dig the tunnels in the first place and to rebuild them—more of them than ever—after they were destroyed.

Impressive determination and defiance on the part of the Palestinians? Maybe, depending on your politics and allegiances. Before they were destroyed, and after they were rebuilt, could it be said that the tunnels were really working? I suppose so, if the only objective was to restore the ability to move products, guns, bombs, and people to places the Israeli enemy did not want these things to go. But in a paradox that often defines violent solutions to violent problems, the tunnels were backfiring, too. A lot of resources and energy were going into their construction, at the expense of schools, for instance. And the tunnels' presence was motivating the Israelis to continue to see Gaza as a violent threat, and to act accordingly.

"Tunneling defies the siege," as one wise writer put it, "yet justifies its continuation."[3]

The destruction of the tunnels, the rebuilding of the tunnels—on and on with the cycle of violence, on and on with the ugly conflict that continues to bring out the worst in both sides. Not for nothing, the United Nations has found both Hamas and the Israelis guilty of serious violations of international humanitarian law and, quite possibly, of war crimes.

Yes, the violence is working so wonderfully.

There is a lesson to be learned in all this, and it's been put to us before: Live by the sword, die by the sword. That's what Jesus said, in essence, in the scene in the Bible where the guards come to take Jesus away, and one of his disciples prepares to fight. Violence begets violence. This you've heard, too, in so many words—most notably from a prophet closer to our own time: Martin Luther King Jr. MLK was not inventing this, of course, but drawing it from the Jesus ethic of nonviolence.

These sages from the ages help us see the price we pay for violent solutions. Look back on recent American history. Think about the methods we have had to deploy to prosecute the war on terrorism. Think of the ways in which we have had to violate the principles of a free and open society in order to *protect* that free and open society.

Okay, I get it. This is the grim reality of the world in which we live. If pacifist idealists were in charge, we would no longer have a free and open society, with laws and due process and democratic principles and all the rest, to protect . . . and subvert. So we can remain grim realists and accept that violence will remain an unfortunate part of our world.

Or we can change our world.

A different world—that's what MLK envisioned. That's the vision Jesus cast. As King said, "Hate begets hate; violence begets violence; toughness begets a greater toughness. We must meet the forces of hate with the power of love. . . . Our aim must never be to defeat or humiliate the white man, but to win his friendship and understanding."[4]

"Love your enemy," Jesus said—a call as mind-blowingly profound as it is unrealistic. It represents a quantum leap in human imagination and a giant step forward in what the philosopher Philip Kitcher describes as the primary, ongoing ethical project of human beings: increasing the amount of responsiveness we have to other people. "When . . . the Jesus of the gospels commands love of our enemies," writes Kitcher, a secularist, "the ideal of responsiveness to others is radically extended. People typically excluded from the ethical conversation are given a presence and a voice."[5]

For us, giving the excluded a presence and a voice would mean that white people in this country see black people in a more empathetic way. It would mean that straight people share the mike with gay people and trans people, that men do the same with women. If we truly want a more peaceful world, we would have to factor into the equation the needs, hopes, and aspirations of those we would rather keep down. And this we must do in our individual hearts, and in the "heart" of society.

Noble idea, you might say. But please. Nonviolence? Maybe in our fantasies. Show me how nonviolence has ever truly *worked* in the rough-and-tumble of real-life human affairs.

Okay.

Fight Fire with . . . Water

If you have seen the movie *Selma*, or if you have read any of the histories of the civil rights movement in this country, you have a sense of how nonviolence can be effective. Examine the philosophies that animated the movement and the tactics used to advance it, and you see something surprising. Nonviolence worked. The nonviolence was shrewd and wily, and its practitioners had to be brave and tough, but the conclusion is inescapable. In helping achieve a major advance in our nation's history, nonviolence carried the day.

Martin Luther King Jr. and his team were not burdened by the availability of force as a viable method for achieving their goal of ending blatant, brutal discrimination against African Americans. It scarcely needs to be said that a violence-based strategy had zero chance of succeeding for them. How freeing. They could be creative. Their tactics could mirror the world they longed to create.

The civil rights movement—we're talking about the MLK branch of it now, not Malcolm X and his "by any means necessary" model—embedded a wily version of Jesus-style nonviolence and, indeed, love at the center of its strategy. Its leaders had the good sense and imagination to adopt the tactic that has often served those through history who have possessed the morally superior idea but have lacked the power to advance it through conventional (i.e., violent) means. MLK and company turned their oppressors' power and immoral philosophies against them.

We know how that played out in the Selma episode and in other key moments: protesters attempting to place their bodies where any white body would be accepted—in a seat at a lunch counter or in the front of the bus, in a voting booth, in a peaceful march—and luring the racist authorities into showing for the whole world what they were really about. What the protesters did, in essence, was frame, highlight, and dramatize the unjust system and the violence that propped it up. The nation was watching on television, and what Americans saw galvanized their consciences. What they saw, of course, was a picture of brave, innocent people being beaten and brutalized. What they saw was the unveiling of a massive injustice that was happening on their watch. They would no longer tolerate it.

Don't mistake nonviolence for weakness. To advance your cause through these tactics requires astonishing amounts of courage and toughness. The civil rights protesters had it. And they showed us this:

Just as water is usually the best way to put out a fire, so, too, is peace the way to quell violence. Peace is the antidote, not more violence. Not more and more and more violence.

This we can learn from Jesus.

For most of my life, I have understood the whole turn-the-other-cheek thing as simple passivity. But in more recent years, my study of Jesus has cast the concept in a different light. If you understand the social context in which Jesus taught, you realize he was promoting a wily form of defiance. He was offering a savvy tactic that bestowed agency, dignity, and equal status on people who, in the eyes of the harsh Roman law, possessed none of these.

In Jesus's time and place, the backhand blow was how superiors put inferiors in their place. When the Romans wanted to show their Jewish subjects who was boss, when masters wanted to remind slaves of who was in charge, when husbands wanted to subjugate their wives, it was often done by means of a backhand slap to the face. You will note that in his teaching Jesus gets specific about which cheek is slapped, and which we are to offer for the second blow. "If anyone slaps you on the right cheek, turn to them the other cheek."

Let's break this down. Given that most people are right-handed, when they administer this backhand blow it's going to land on the recipient's right cheek. Business as usual. Here's where it gets interesting, and daring. By responding with the offer of his or her left cheek, the inferior-status person has put the superior in an awkward position. A dismissive backhand is no longer possible. The oppressor is presented with a prospect that comes in the guise of submissiveness but is actually quite assertive.

As the late theologian Walter Wink put it: "The left cheek now offers a perfect target for a blow with the right fist; but only equals fought with fists, as we know from Jewish sources, and the last thing the master wishes to do is to establish this underling's equality."

Jesus, Wink goes on to say, is encouraging victims to "stand up for yourselves, defy your masters, assert your humanity; but don't answer the oppressor in kind. Find a new, third way that is neither cowardly submission nor violent reprisal."[6]

Something similar is in play in the Jesus teaching about "going the second mile," as we often hear it phrased, and in the Jesus teaching about what to do if someone sues you for your tunic. Give him the damn tunic, Jesus says—and your cloak, too.

Seriously?

The "second mile" teaching is from the Sermon on the Mount, where Jesus says, "And whoever compels you to go one mile, go with him two." While we often think of the "second mile" teaching as encouragement to be more generous—and, indeed, the teaching works at this level—it's fair to say that Jesus is also at his subversive best here. The key word is *compel.* In Jesus's time and place, Roman soldiers could compel the conquered civilians to drop whatever they were doing and go to work for them. This often took the form of carrying soldiers' heavy loads as they marched through your village. By custom, this form of temporary conscription had a limit. It was understood that you, the humble Jewish villager, would have to carry the soldier's pack no more than one mile.

With Wink's help once again, let's look closely at what is happening: You and the soldier who appropriated you have reached the one-mile mark. He fully expects you to stop now, unburden yourself of his heavy pack, and go back to what you were doing. He probably expects you to be grumpy about it, passive-aggressive, keen on demonstrating your displeasure without being so confrontational as to tempt him to punish you. But you defy his expectation and mess with his mind. Cheerily, you say, "I'll keep going." The soldier is surprised. He is thrown off, worried. Are you trying to trap him in an infraction? Will he get in trouble with his superiors if he lets you break the one-mile rule? Are you mocking his strength? Are you actually enjoying the experience of carrying his stuff and, thus, depriving him of the gratification of forcing you to do something you do not want to do? Wink writes:

> From a situation of servile impressment, the oppressed have once more seized the initiative. They have taken back the power of choice. They have thrown the soldier off balance by depriving him of the predictability of his victim's response. He has never dealt with such a problem before. Now he must make a decision for which nothing in his previous experience has prepared him. If he has enjoyed feeling superior to the vanquished, he will not enjoy it today. Imagine a Roman infantryman pleading with a Jew to give back his pack! The humor of this scene may have escaped us, but it could scarcely have been lost on Jesus's hearers, who must have been delighted at the prospect of thus discomfiting their oppressors.[7]

As for the tunic-and-cloak teaching, this, too, works as a summons to be supergenerous. And it, too, has a subversive element. Here, Jesus is again showing oppressed people a way to mess with their oppressors' minds, to turn their power against them, and to shame them for their inhumane behavior. Understand the context: Burdensome debt was a systematic problem for poor Jews in Jesus's time. This was not a result of these people being irresponsible or lazy but a predictable outcome of a system of onerous taxes and interest rates that drove many day laborers and tenant farmers into desperate economic straits. Creditors were often taking debtors to court, Walter Wink explains, and sometimes the peasant's only possession, his only collateral, was, quite literally, the clothing on his back.

Imagine the scene: By custom and law, a creditor could seize a debtor's garment and hold it as collateral. So you, the debtor who has been confronted by your creditor, take off your tunic and hand it over, leaving you with only your cloak to cover your nakedness. You say, "You have taken my land, you have taken my money, you have taken my tunic, you have taken my pride—why not take *everything*?" You hand over your cloak. And there you stand, naked. What we have, suddenly, is a spectacle—a protest. Your nakedness poses a problem for your creditor not only because this scene is attracting attention, framing his cruelty in a harsh light, but because your nakedness shames him. Nakedness, as Wink points out, "was taboo in Judaism, and shame fell less on the naked party than on the person viewing or causing the nakedness."[8]

You have shamed both the oppressor and the unjust system.

The gospels record other compelling examples of Jesus rejecting the usual binary choices—aggression or submission, condemnation or endorsement, fight or flight—and devising a creative Plan C.

Nowhere does he do it with greater genius than in the famous situation where he is asked to give his opinion on what ought to be done about the woman who is caught in the act of adultery. As told in John 8, the authorities have roped Jesus into a situation where the two obvious options available to him are bad; the Pharisees are laying a trap. The interaction may look innocent enough on the surface. It seems as if they are honoring Jesus's knowledge and moral authority and asking his advice. Not so. If he cites the ancient law and advises death by stoning, he will be stepping out of line and asserting a form of religious authority he does not officially possess. But if he demurs, he will appear to be tolerating an intolerable sin. He is damned if he does and damned if he doesn't.

Wily Jesus does not step into the trap. He evades it and humbles the would-be setters of the trap in one brilliant move, uttering his famous line: "Let him who is without sin cast the first stone." Dumbfounded, the accusers slowly drift away.

Jesus has defused a tense situation dripping with the prospect of violence.

World at War

But what about the real world? we ask. What about situations like World War II? Are we going to turn our other cheeks to *Hitler*? And terrorism—if terrorists are storming in to blow up the White House, are we going to shame them by taking off our cloaks? Or are we going to do what's necessary and stop them in their tracks—dead?

I get it. I really do. But the Jesus ethic is more applicable here than we might realize. Let's consider World War II, which is often held up, and rightfully so, as an example of a necessary and successful war for the Allies. We will do so by first taking up the aftermath of World War I.

A boot on the throat—this was, in the experience of the vanquished Germans, the effect of the Treaty of Versailles following World War I. The Germans had finally been defeated at an enormous cost. And then, as if to ensure they would not rise up militarily again, draconian surrender terms were slapped on.

We know how that worked out.

Now, by contrast, think about how the United States and its allies dealt with the defeated Germans and Japanese following World War II. For a moment, transport your mind past the mind-boggling bloodshed that occurred during the war and contemplate what happened when the fighting ended: Did we keep our enemies down? Did we permanently take over their countries? Did we keep our boot on their throats? We did the opposite, actually. We helped them rebuild their countries and economies, and they went on to become models of prosperity and nonmilitarism. Over the seventy years that have followed, both have been prosperous and peaceful and great friends of the United States.

Nonviolence worked.

If Jesus Were in Charge

If Jesus were in charge, nonviolence success stories would not even *be* stories; they would just be the regular state of affairs. The situation calls to mind a famous quotation from the English writer and lay theologian G. K. Chesterton, who observed, "The Christian ideal has not been tried and found wanting; it has been found difficult and left untried."[9]

Since Constantine, the world has had many (putative) Christians in charge of various kingdoms and sundry lands. But never Jesus. We have seen Jesus-style nonviolence at work in some shining moments, however.

Like when . . . a Chinese man stood up to a column of tanks near Beijing's Tiananmen Square, shielded only by the tank operators' unwillingness to crush him, framing, for a brief but unforgettable moment, the power of simple human decency to thwart superior military might.

Like when . . . Mohandas Gandhi leveraged the force of his moral credibility and his willingness to starve himself to get the British rulers to drop their support for a constitutional provision that would have reinforced the inferiority of India's lowest caste, the so-called untouchables.

Like when . . . Martin Luther King Jr., believing that it would eventually cost him his life, continued to press hard truth on the American conscience by nonviolent means, refusing to hate his people's oppressors, and instead holding up the faith that inside each one of us, even in the heart of our enemy, there still exists the possibility of goodness and the longing for justice.

Like when . . . Jesus let the authorities crucify him, providing history with an unforgettably dramatic example of what it means to sacrifice oneself for the benefit of others, and for the sake of the superior moral ideal.

Earlier we talked about the use of nonviolent action to "frame" and dramatize inhumane behaviors and cruel social situations that our consciences cannot tolerate. We can see Jesus on the cross as one of Western history's ultimate framings. And even if we don't believe the literal truth of the next part of the story, we can accept Jesus's resurrection as a powerfully truthful symbol. The ideal of peace and justice could not be defeated then, and cannot be defeated now.

When we think about the world that is, in so many ways, disappointing and depressing, it seems sadly appropriate that the man who insisted that we must not dehumanize *anyone* was terminated by leaders of a system that depended on dehumanization to perpetuate itself and prop up the power and privilege of those who benefited.

Well, they may have killed the messenger, but they didn't kill the message.

Breaking the Cycle

The nonviolent message of Jesus reverberated in my thoughts when I read a statement from the American Humanist Association following the murder of nine black people at their church in Charleston, South Carolina, in 2015. It read, "While we bemoan the current state of our world, we humanists must hold on to the evidence-based hope that empathy and compassion will win over violence and hate." We could hear the Jesus message echoing loudly when the sister of one of the Charleston victims stood before the shooter in the courtroom a few days after his murderous rampage and forgave him. Afterward she explained that, yes, she was very angry, but that her sister had taught her that "we are the family that love built. We have no room for hating."

If ever we saw the deadly consequences of no empathy,

no compassion, it was in the killer, a young white supremacist who sat with his eventual victims in a Bible study session at their church for an hour before pulling out his gun. He reportedly said later that he received such a warm welcome, was treated with such kindness during that hour, he was tempted to reconsider. Tragically, his hateful ideology overruled what his eyes and ears were telling him about the decency and humanity of his victims. "You rape our women and you're taking over our country," he reportedly told them as he loaded, "and you have to go."

We must break the cycle of violence the way Jesus broke it at the Garden of Gethsemane when he ordered his disciple to put away his sword. It's not as unrealistic as it seems.

When grieving family members confronted the Charleston shooter at the courthouse a few days later, it would have been quite understandable had one or more shouted hateful epithets at him, perhaps even lunged at him. Revenge is par for the course. What these people did, by contrast, was demonstrate the kind of change our world needs in order to evolve up and out of the cycle of violence. With the eyes of the world on them, they forgave the hate-filled shooter who took away their loved ones. By expunging the need for retaliation from their hearts, they broke the cycle of violence, at least in that moment, in that place.

So it will have to go if the ethic of peace is to prevail in our violent world. So it will have to go if we as individuals, religious or secular, are to achieve a more peaceful state of affairs in our minds and hearts. Changes in laws might help achieve increments of progress toward peace; I, for one, would welcome them. But ultimately, it's an inside-out transformation we need. Like that evoked by the Charleston mourners. Like the one imagined by Jesus when he famously said: "Blessed are the peacemakers."

A few days after Charleston, one of my frequent correspondents e-mailed with a question related to the column I had published about the massacre. He resonated with my comments about the violence and racism afflicting our society, and with my call for healing. But what could be done, he asked, to achieve this healing?

I don't have a detailed blueprint for how to build a violence-free world. But I do see a way forward. As I told my correspondent then, and as I'll suggest to you now, that way is the way of Jesus. If it's a peaceful world you desire—and this holds, I'm convinced, even if you don't typically find yourself trafficking in Jesus ideas—listen to Jesus. Watch Jesus. Implement Jesus.

Chapter Three

SEXPLOITATION

It's like ordering Seamless. But you're ordering a person.[1]

—A user of the hookup app Tinder, comparing it to the meal-delivery service popular in his city

Sex is broken.

Oh, I know. Sex is the most wonderful thing in the world. Perhaps the most important, too. So we are told by countless culture messages. If you're lucky, maybe that's how sex has been in your life: a source of joy, an expression and enhancement of your loving, romantic relationships.

But for many, including the gallingly high percentage of women who have been raped or subjected to other forms of sexual violence, sex is not the most wonderful thing in the world. For them, sex is a source of pain—pain of both the physical and the psychological varieties. For many men, especially those caught up in compulsive consumption of pornography and serial "conquests," sex is wonderful like heroin is wonderful. It seems great in the moment. But it's killing you—part of you, at least—and hurting those around you.

To be sure, if you are gay, today's sexual environment

is infinitely better than what we had in the past—a society that shamed and pathologized loves and attractions that did not fit the majority playbook, causing incalculable suffering and untold damage among those who had those attractions. If you are a woman, today's environment is better in many ways, too. Women enjoy far more sexual freedom than they once did, and more authority over their sexual and reproductive decisions.

Unfortunately, though, we have a hard time behaving well when it comes to sex. We glorify sex. We sell sex. We use sex. We exploit sex, and the people from whom sex can be procured. And because we blow sex out of proportion—and by "we" I am mostly talking about those of my gender, the heterosexual men—we often blow the sex parts of women's bodies out of proportion, too. This has the effect of shrinking everything else about women that ought to be honored—you know, other parts of their bodies, and their nonphysical endowments, like their intelligence, their dignity, their humanity.

Sex: one of the most amazing things about being human.

Sex: the thing that so often leads us to treat others in *de*humanizing ways.

Men Behaving Badly

Whether you conceive the "creator" to be God or evolution, you will probably agree that he, she, or it complicated things in making sex so alluring and then tangling it up not just with reproduction but with the power differential between men and women. Not just the physical power that correlates with men commonly being larger and more muscled than women, but the cultural and political advantages men have enjoyed in most cultures, through most of history. Especially for women, the complication creates problems on the sex and gender-relations fronts.

In Argentina, a culture of machismo prevails. As the *New York Times* reports, "Argentine men feel entitled to deliver a public 'piropo'—literally, a compliment; in practice, any lewd comment or wolf whistle—to any woman of their choosing. What may once have been a tradition of poetic gallantry has degenerated into crude catcalling and aggressive propositioning. Such routine street harassment is widely regarded as socially acceptable, a masculine right even."[2]

But it gets worse. A trend of femicide murders in Argentina has been playing out in recent years, instances of men and boys killing their wives and ex-wives, their girlfriends and ex-girlfriends, by bullets, knives, even burning. By the count of a nonprofit organization that provides shelter for abuse victims, hundreds of women a year are being killed by the men in their lives.[3]

Only in Argentina? When you read the headlines, follow the "conversations" happening online, and really think about it, you realize the dynamic in this country is not so different.

Entitlement—the misbegotten sense that women and their bodies in some sense belong to men—often lurks behind male sexual aggression. When men are hearing and seeing, over and over and over, that sex is great, that lots of people are having lots of sex, perhaps it's inevitable that some men will be infuriated by the fact that they are not getting any. No doubt, their sense of the ubiquity and awesomeness of all the sex out there is exaggerated. Nonetheless, desire morphs into entitlement, which morphs into resentment, which morphs into anger, which morphs into aggression, which morphs, in worst-case scenarios, to rape and to . . .

> *Men are afraid women will laugh at them. Women are afraid men will kill them.*[4]

In the Santa Barbara area, one young man began to feel so angry about his lack of sex that he built up a rage against women for not giving it to him, and against the men who presumably were getting it. This twenty-two-year-old uploaded a video to YouTube before he started killing people, laying out his plan and describing his burning desire to punish women for rejecting him. (Given the indiscriminate nature of the shootings, it's clear that in his calculations any women would do as stand-ins for the ones who spurned him.) He injured fourteen people that day and killed six people—four men, two women—before shooting himself.

Not so different were the killings at a Pittsburgh area gym. This frustrated man used a website to catalog the rejections and sexual frustrations that built up for him before a shooting spree at a women's aerobics class. He injured nine people and killed three women before he shot himself.

Extreme, isolated examples, you might say. Surely the situation is not as dire as might be suggested by these random acts of angry lunatics. I wish I could agree. But a survey of the wider landscape finds damage all around—most of it less dramatic, yes, but damage just the same.

Take rape and sexual assault. A recent poll found that more than 20 percent of women students at a sampling of promiment universities in the United States report being sexually assaulted. This survey, released by the *Washington Post* and Kaiser Family Foundation in 2015,[5] vindicates earlier surveys that yielded similar results but were scoffed at by many critics as wildly exaggerated. Unless you're ready to prove that there is a coordinated conspiracy by young women to lie and exaggerate about this matter, it's impossible to escape the conclusion that too many college men are using force to get women to have sex with them.

We see many other forms of sexual abuse and exploitation out on that landscape, in America and around the world: Poor young women being trapped in sexual slavery, their bodies sold to strangers in need of an orifice. Popular entertainment vehicles like the HBO series *Game of Thrones* spiking episodes with gratuitous, graphic rape scenes that leave us a little uncertain about whether we are supposed to feel horrified, titillated, or both. Magazines and other forms of popular culture sending the message, over and over and over, that women's bodies are for men's visual and physical pleasure, and that a woman's value correlates with her ability to align her dimensions, shape, and behavior with a standard that was apparently concocted by horny fourteen-year-old boys. Men and women discarding spouses and partners when the narcotic high of sex and romance wears off, as if these onetime lovers were just more consumer products that could be traded in for new models. Wealthy and powerful men flashing their status by strutting in public with their young, hot "trophy wives."

Even if a girl or woman is not one of the sexual assault

statistics, she must go through life in this environment. This is the headwind she faces, the current against which she swims, as she tries to establish a life of dignity. And for the roles they play in perpetrating and participating in these damaging aspects of our sex culture, I posit that men's lives are impoverished, too.

My diagnosis of our culture's sex dysfunction focuses on heterosexual men because it's they who hold the power over these matters, for the most part, and it's they who drive so much of the dehumanizing dynamic we find on the sex-and-culture landscape.[6] There is also the fact that the straight menfolk are my gender, which by my way of thinking gives me greater right to criticize and a better perspective from which to do it.

Here's acknowledgment to the men who generally behave well in these areas. The finger is not pointing at you. But we can probably all do more to challenge aspects of sex culture that are hurting people.

Which brings us to Jesus.

You might wonder, of course, what we could possibly learn about sex and gender relations from an ostensibly celibate religious figure from two thousand years ago, way before we had online pornography and reliable contraception and the other things that define sex culture today. He was part of a pious religious community with sexual mores so restrictive as to make America's supposedly hallowed age of Beaver Cleaver and *Father Knows Best* look libertine. His story was propagated by a sect so detached from the here and now and so convinced of an imminent apocalypse that it advised members to abandon any notion of marriage and family. You might also point out that Jesus comes wrapped up in a Christendom that sports a spotty-at-best record when it comes to healthy understandings of sex. When we try to figure out what is broken about sex today, and how we could go about repairing it, surely, you might say, there is little about Jesus that could be relevant or helpful.

But please stay with me. Let me show you how the Jesus story, the Jesus example, and the Jesus way speak directly to broken sex today, and can help us arrive at a much-needed mending.

Sex and Jesus

It's true that Jesus did not talk a lot about sex. For example, on one of today's hottest-button sex issues, homosexuality, Jesus is silent.[7] But while his body of work might not be extensive when it comes to sex, we can profit from a close look at what he *is* reported to have said about sex and related issues in the Bible. Two areas he did address remain top of mind in our place and time: divorce and adultery.

At first glance (and maybe on second, third, and fourth, too) a lot of us aren't going to like Jesus's divorce teaching. In the Sermon on the Mount, he declares:

> It has been said, "Anyone who divorces his wife must give her a certificate of divorce. But I tell you that anyone who divorces his wife, except for sexual immorality, makes her the victim of adultery, and anyone who marries a divorced woman commits adultery."

Basic idea: Divorce is wrong, declares Jesus. People should not get divorced unless their spouses have been having sex with other people.

What, pray tell, are we twenty-first-century people to do with *this*?

Like many Jesus teachings, this one establishes an ideal. If we factor this ideal into our moral calculations, if we hold it in tension with the messy realities and decisions before us, some useful, healthy, and doable possibilities emerge.

For one: If we are considering getting divorced, we need to contemplate the human consequences—for our spouses, our children, our communities, and ourselves. And if we do it, we'd better have a damn good reason. Being bored or annoyed with our current spouse, and being attracted to someone else, does not constitute that damn good reason.

Pope Francis, one of the better Jesus explainers and implementors in our time, brings something helpful to this conversation. Marital separation, Francis has said, is sometimes "morally necessary" to protect children. A member of the elite club of people who grew up with out-of-control alcoholic fathers, I can testify to the logic and righteousness of this claim, and the necessity of divorce in some circumstances. Despite her strict Catholic upbringing and despite divorce being relatively rare and stigmatizing at the time—it was the early 1960s—my mother got a divorce to save my sisters and me, and herself, from having to live with destructive behavior every day. Thank goodness. To state the obvious, this moral necessity is present, too, when one spouse is repeatedly physically or psychologically abusive to the other spouse or the children. Play this out, and you will no doubt see other situations where the end of a marriage is, as Francis puts it, "morally necessary."

In what Jesus says about divorce, I see a strong respect-for-women element. The way he phrases the teaching ("Anyone who divorces his wife . . ."), it's clear he's addressing the men in the audience. Recall that in Jesus's time and place, women were virtually powerless, treated more like property than like people; recall that wives were royally screwed financially and in every other way if their husbands discarded them. From this view it's really quite impressive to find Jesus having unusually compassionate and power-balanced dealings with women, very much against the grain of social norms. It's striking to find him sticking up for women again and again—as he does here, and as we saw earlier, when he rescues the woman who is on the verge of being stoned to death for adultery. On the issue of divorce, it's as if he is saying to anyone who might be entertaining notions of greener pastures to stop for a moment and think of the human consequences. If you split up with your spouse so you can start screwing someone new, who else is going to get "screwed" in the deal?

The children are certainly among them. Here again, I have membership in a club of sorts—the Children of Divorced Parents Club, you might call it—that gives me useful perspective. Divorce is no picnic for the kids. Obviously, the single-parent environment is sometimes vastly preferable to the one that would prevail had mother and father stayed together. Yet still . . . would some of the holes in my game as an adult be a little less gaping if I'd had the steady, healthy presence of a father who could show me good ways to handle situations, to fix stuff, to fish? So, too, am I a member of the large group of Parents Who Have Been Divorced. How would my daughter's childhood have been better if her mother and I had not parted ways so soon after her arrival? The statistical evidence backs what my personal experience and observations suggest. Not that single-parent families are any less deserving of respect and support. Not that the products of these homes are defective. Not that marital strife and conflict are good for the couple's children. But the health-and-success metrics for children of divorce do tend to be somewhat poorer than for those who grow up in two-parent homes.[8]

And what of adultery? In his Sermon on the Mount, Jesus seems to rubber-stamp the long-standing moral law against adultery, as if no further elaboration is required. Couple that with his exhortation to the adulterer to "sin no more," and you have an unambiguous picture of Jesus opposing selfish and irresponsible sexual choices. (It is interesting to note that most Americans today are with him on this. Polling data show that even as we have become more accepting of premarital sex and same-sex relationships, the majority of us remain opposed to cheating on our spouses.)[9]

No surprises or ambiguities so far. But now we come to the Jesus teaching that sets many of us to head scratching: the weird part about men who "lust" for women.

> You have heard that it was said, "You shall not commit adultery." But I tell you that anyone who looks at a woman lustfully has already committed adultery with her in his heart.

This is, as I say, weird—and humbling, too, for those of us who are able to keep our pants on and want to feel a little superior about that. Similar to his teaching that we should love our haters, Jesus's comment here reminds us of the new philosophical paradigm ushered in by him and those who built a religion around him—one that shifts the focus of moral evaluations from rules and behavior to our interior worlds, to the contents of our hearts.

When it comes to sex, what are we to make of this? Most heterosexual, married men do indeed notice women's attractiveness, and when we do, we feel a charge of something that is quite different from what we experience if we notice a handsome man walking past. Does this make us adulterers? And if we're breaking the rules anyway—why not just go all the way and break those rules with our bodies, too?

Lust is more than looking, notes the Christian writer Amy R. Buckley. "It is different from feeling attraction or involuntary sexual arousal. Lust entails seeing another's body as an object for self-gratification. It defines the person not as a human, created in the image of God, but as a means of carnal pleasure."[10]

By naming the inclinations of the human heart—and surfacing the link between seemingly harmless desires and hurtful consequences—Jesus points us in a better direction: He challenges us to "look" differently, to value appropriately. Only then can we choose to see others as they really are—as whole persons of inestimable worth—and treat them as they deserve to be treated.

So, yes, on this issue of how we men look at women, Jesus had a point that remains amazingly relevant today.

Boys Will Be Boys?

The way some men talk about these things, it's as if lustful thoughts cannot be helped. Boys, after all, will be boys. Women have to help us out here, they say, by being modest in their behavior and dress and, better yet, by simply being absent from the premises when men must really concentrate. This view is especially prevalent in religion's more conservative precincts.

When I was still living in Portland, I once accepted an invitation from the chaplain of the college where I worked to join a group of students and him for a visit to a local mosque. The mosque director was genuinely engaging and amiable during the Q & A, winning us over with his witty anecdotes and movie references. But when one of the female students in our group asked him why men and women worship separately at his mosque, as at most, his answer struck me as immature, even a little prurient. When women are present, he explained, their physical attractiveness makes it difficult for the men to focus on worship. And he proceeded to tell us, as if we would find it amusing and persuasive, that when he is out with his wife in public, she has to monitor how long his eyes linger on some of the scenery, like, say, a nicely shaped woman runner in tight-fitting clothes. This, he seemed to suggest, is just how things are with respect to men and women.

But is it? Are we to believe that men have no impulse control? That women and men must therefore be segregated—often, let's face it, at the expense of the women?

Nonsense. And, furthermore, potentially dangerous. There

is a direct line between this reassignment of responsibility and the convenient shifting of blame that we often see when women are victims of rape or other forms of sexual aggression. If the woman's shape or clothing choices are just a bit too appealing, some men say, if she was drinking, if she was "in the wrong place at the wrong time," then she asked for it—and the perpetrator is largely innocent.

As a world, as a culture, as individuals, we need to grow up in these matters. We must, I propose, treat women the way Jesus did.

It's really quite impressive and instructive when you watch him in the gospel accounts. The stories make it clear that women were part of the Jesus community and were among the people he called friends. Jesus was downright profligate at times in his extension of love, warmth, and acceptance to women, even to women of questionable reputation. He would have been within his rights and the cultural norms of his time to have excluded women from his ministry altogether, or kept them at a "safer" distance. Doing so certainly would have made him less conspicuous in the eyes of the authorities who had it in for him.

Consider the story in Luke 7 about the "sinful" woman with the jar of perfume and you'll see what I mean.

Here's the scene: Jesus is part of a gathering at the home of a Pharisee, a member of an all-male, highly respected religious group. Jesus is seated. His feet are dirty and, likely, sore and tired from the day's walking. His host has not done Jesus the courtesy of giving him a chance to wash those dirty feet. Nor has the host had one of his servants attend to it, as would be the custom with an important guest.

A woman enters uninvited. The locals recognize her

as someone of poor reputation—a prostitute, we are led to believe. They are aghast to find her approaching Jesus. Something about him is deeply moving to her, and she begins to weep. Noticing his feet have not been washed, she kneels, and begins to use her tears to cleanse them. Then she wipes his feet with her hair, applies perfume to them, and kisses them.

The Pharisee is affronted. If Jesus were truly a prophet, he grouses, he would have known who this woman was, and would certainly *not* have allowed this transgressive intimacy. Instead, Jesus has allowed her near, receiving her humble service.

What a strangely moving moment has unfolded! The picture of this nameless, outcast woman, this persona non grata, washing and kissing the traveling prophet's feet might strike us as subservience, but I don't think that view does the story justice. We can see that the woman's act is willingly offered, and deeply heartfelt. By receiving her care, Jesus seems to be vouching for her humanity, her dignity. And he does so with full knowledge that it will rub some important people the wrong way.

Jesus is aware of the Pharisee's censure, so he asks his host a simple but searing question: "Do you see this woman?"

I read that as Jesus saying to the Pharisee: Are you willing to see only a stock character, a function, an object? Or can you see the real, live, multidimensional human being she is, whatever her profession?[11]

Jesus, with his stubborn insistence on seeing humanity even where it might be hardest to find, tended to stick up for prostitutes. These women of ill repute, he declared, had moral standing superior to that of the pious but judgmental

Pharisees. As the religion scholar Harvey Cox points out, Jesus was able to see prostitutes and their circumstances in a deeper, more compassionate way than both those who judged them and those who used them. He could see that prostitutes in his time (not unlike ours) were generally pressured into their occupation by poverty, trafficking, and other factors that left them little choice.[12]

In the interaction between Jesus and the woman of ill repute that day, lines of authority and status were crossed—lines of gender, too. And something transgressively beautiful happened.

Buying and Selling

You will be hard-pressed to find much beauty in the scene that unfolds countless times every day when a man sits in front of his computer and watches actors playing out someone's crude sex fantasy. Online pornography is extremely popular in the United States. By one report, the Internet's porn sites draw more traffic than Netflix, Twitter, and Amazon combined.[13] That figure has been challenged, yet even so, there is no denying the reach and influence of the multibillion-dollar pornography industry. A recent Pew Research Center study finds that among Americans who use the Internet to watch videos, 25 percent of men (and 8 percent of women) say they access porn.[14]

The feminist writer Naomi Wolf, among others, has articulated why it's not just old-biddy prudes and Bible-thumping preachers who ought to have something to say about the ubiquity and nature of today's porn. The version of sex being promoted is grossly distorted, degrading, and, ultimately, deadening, Wolf writes—deadening to the ability to appreciate the comparatively boring sex that most people have in real life, and deadening to the human spirit that one would hope to find celebrated in the sex that is being had by real people.

Wolf notes that many women today face unrelenting and impossible pressure to live up to the expectations of their porn-jaded men.

> Being naked is not enough; you have to be buff, be tan with no tan lines, have the surgically hoisted breasts and the Brazilian bikini wax—just like porn stars. (In my gym, the forty-year-old women have adult pubic hair; the twenty-somethings have all been trimmed and styled.) Pornography is addictive; the baseline gets ratcheted up. By the new millennium, a vagina—which, by the way, used to have a pretty high "exchange value," as Marxist economists would say—wasn't enough; it barely registered on the thrill scale. All mainstream porn—and certainly the Internet—made routine use of all available female orifices.[15]

As Wolf asks, is this what sexual liberation is supposed to be? "Or is it the case," she writes, "that the relationship between the multi-billion-dollar porn industry, compulsiveness, and sexual appetite has become like the relationship between agribusiness, processed foods, supersize portions, and obesity?"

Men expecting their girlfriends to perform like porn stars.

Men feeling blasé and judgmental about the real women in bed with them. Women feeling devalued, insecure, and under threat. Relationships subverted and sabotaged by the drive-by business of fantasy sex. These and more, it seems to me, are the tolls exacted by the often "free" porn available today.

In the midst of all this degradation and confusion, perhaps we should not be surprised to learn about the chant overheard or brandished on signs at a couple of universities, where groups of men have declared: "No means yes! Yes means anal!"[16]

This is how sex is supposed to be?

For an answer, we should consult with those who pay the price, directly and indirectly, for sex as it is today. Among them: the trafficked, the raped, the abused, the exploited, the betrayed, the deserted. Also among them: the abandoned and neglected children of parents in name only, who were up for sex but not for its reproductive consequences,[17] emblematic of an irresponsibility that, sadly, has gone hand in hand with a sexual revolution that was in so many ways overdue, but that lost part of its best self at some crossroads between then and now.

Toward a More Humane and Healthy Future

Those of us who fancy ourselves sophisticated, liberal, and enlightened about sex may feel especially conflicted in this conversation. None of us would be caught dead sounding prudish. This is an age when we're supposed to be up for anything as far as sex is concerned. Yet "anything" keeps changing. As Wolf notes, and as I have learned from conversations, it's cool now for women to go to strip clubs, for instance. Some have told me they do it for irony's sake; some, to show how open-minded they are; some, because "the women are hot." Part of our credo as liberals is that it's all okay, as long as no one is getting hurt.

Personally, I'm glad we have that "no one is getting hurt" element in our calculus. The problem is our slowness to see, and reluctance to admit, the many ways in which sex today *is* hurting people. Take strip clubs. Even if we don't think it's degrading for the women who work at these places, how do we come to terms with the knowledge that some of these establishments are outposts in an underground trafficking network, meaning that the dancers are, quite possibly, slaves being sold out by profit-hungry men?[18]

If calling these things out makes us sound prudish, maybe more of us should be willing to sound like prudes.

The *New York Times* columnist Ross Douthat, a Catholic conservative, can sound prudish when he writes about today's sex culture. But he's got a point when he says that the sexual revolution has evolved into something that's not liberal so much as libertine. A sex revolution that was supposed to be liberating, empowering, and healthy has morphed into something that too often looks twisted, disempowering, and *un*healthy. He writes:

> Viewed from another angle, that same revolution looks more like a permission slip for the strong and privileged to prey upon the weak and easily exploited. This is the sexual revolution of Hugh Hefner and Larry Flynt and Joe Francis and roughly 98 percent

> of the online pornography consumed by young men. It's the revolution that's been better for fraternity brothers than their female guests, better for the rich than the poor, better for the beautiful than the plain, better for liberated adults than fatherless children . . . and so on down a long, depressing list.[19]

When we think about what is damaging and dehumanizing in today's sex culture, we might be tempted to devise a way to go back to the (presumably) better days of old. But there is no going back. And let's not forget that any supposedly innocent age was not so innocent for many.

Better to go forward toward a more humane and healthy sexual future, asking, among other questions, how the way of Jesus could contribute to our success in that venture. In my view, Jesus does not have much to offer if the conversation is going to be the stuff teased on the covers of the health and fashion magazines. But when we're ready to recognize the damage wrought by our greedy obsession with "getting" and "having" sex, just like another consumer commodity, and when we're willing to rethink an exploitation-and-gratification model that is leaving untold casualties along the way, then, arguably, there are few who have *more* to offer than Jesus.

Although he did not coin the phrase, it's worth noting that Jesus famously taught his followers to do unto others as we would want done unto us. I wonder what would happen if we plugged *that* into the sex formula. Jesus emphasized, too, the imperative to love our fellow human beings, whoever they are, and he modeled history's preeminent example of *love at great personal cost.*

What happens when you inject a shot of *that* into sex culture today?

You get something I believe most of us would want if we really thought about it and summoned the wiser parts of our minds: a sex culture that might come up short at times in below-the-belt gratification but that would greatly reduce the casualty count. We would get a sex culture in which far fewer are being used and abused for someone's pleasure, and far more are experiencing the joys of physical intimacy in the safety and dignity of a loving, egalitarian relationship. We would get a sex culture in which the sex that's being had is consistently more edifying to the human spirit.

I don't know exactly what this humanizing ethic would look like for each of us. I don't know what it would mean, exactly, in terms of the numbers and genders of the sex partners we would have, and whether we would stay with our current partners when we are tempted to go. I don't know how it would play out, precisely, with each of us with respect to our reproductive and contraceptive practices.

But I do know that if we took our cue from the great humanizer, if we let Jesus point us in the right direction, sex culture would radically change for the better. If we heeded the Jesus voice, sex would become healthier and more humane, more responsible, and more respectful. Happier, on the whole, for all concerned.

Especially those at whose expense we "enjoy" sex as it is today.

Chapter Four

HIGH ANXIETY

I know what I would have done had I been there with the disciples that day. I would have been stressing out and wringing my hands, sputtering, "Jesus Christ! How the hell are we going to feed all these people?"

That experience of stress—and its antidote—are captured in a fascinating story told in all four canonical gospels. Allow me to set the stage, drawing mainly from John's account:

Jesus has been sent reeling with horrific news. His beloved mentor, John the Baptist, has been executed—beheaded, actually, on a whim of the daughter of King Herod's wife. Desperately needing solitude and room to grieve, Jesus attempts to steal away by taking a boat to what he hopes will be a secluded location. But no such luck. Word of his whereabouts quickly spreads, and before long, a huge crowd has caught up with him.

So Jesus shifts gears. He begins to teach, heal, and interact with the people. All day, the crowd keeps growing.

By afternoon, the head count stands at five thousand or thereabouts—and that's just the men.

Now some of the disciples urgently advise Jesus to send people away so they can get busy scrounging up dinner for themselves in the nearby villages. Surely, they hope, Jesus isn't going to put it on them, the disciples, to figure out how to feed everyone! Still, perhaps anticipating that Jesus might get some crazy notion, they conduct an inventory and establish that the only food on hand is in a boy's basket. He has five loaves of bread and two fishes.

About then, Jesus coyly asks the disciple Philip what he thinks ought to be done. "Where shall we buy bread for these people to eat?"

Wait. *What?*

"It would take more than half a year's wages," Philip protests, "to buy enough bread for each one to have a bite!"

Oh, Philip, Jesus must be thinking. *Please chill. We'll figure something out.*

Nervous Nation

The details and setting vary today, but I would venture that all of us can identify with Philip's reaction when demands far outstrip resources. It's likely that at no time in history have we been so aware of the debilitating effects of stress and anxiety—yet so powerless to escape their grip. But here, too, the counterintuitive ways of Jesus under pressure suggest the very remedies we most need, both as individuals and as a society.

When I read the literature on anxiety in our society, I

have no problem relating. Maybe because there was a lot of negative drama in my life when I was a kid, or maybe because I'm just naturally high-strung, I am always worried about what could go wrong.

My friends in high school picked up on my preternatural jitters. Whatever scheme was being cooked up for fun at a given moment, I always had a million questions: How are we going to get there? Who else is going? What if this happens? What if that happens? Fortunately, my friend Ron had the exact opposite disposition. He would put on a serene expression, pat me on the shoulder, and say in an obnoxiously happy voice, "Tommy, it's going to be *perfectly okay*!" Pat, pat.

When weed smoking was on the fun agenda in college, my friends would get high from the stuff. Me? I'd get worried.

Maybe it's like that for you, too. I still struggle to believe it's going to be *perfectly okay* when I start running scenarios through my head. The combination of time (there's not much of it) and things to get done (the list seems infinite) puts me on edge. So does money. Where are the funds going to come from to pay off the loans and go on that trip we've been planning? How are we going to cover moving expenses *and* the massive car-repair bill? Retirement? At what stage of *that* game are we going to run out of money and resort to dog food?

Questions. Doubts. Fretting over the times I decided to "wing it" only to regret it later. It hasn't helped that the main profession I've had over the years, communications and media relations, is one where it pays to conjure up the worst-case scenarios and play them out. I call it being professionally paranoid. If our institution is facing a tough situation and decides on Solution A, what kind of flak is that going to bring from the cynics and critics? If we continue to do nothing about Problem B, how might that blow up on us and our reputation? If we respond to a media situation by sending out Message C, how might it be misconstrued or deliberately twisted to make us look bad?

In my line of work, this is called doing your job. Ride this train too deeply into the rest of your life, however, and it will transport you straight to the therapist's office or the pharmacy.

Unfortunately, I am not alone. Almost one in five of us suffers from some kind of anxiety disorder, and as many as a third of us go through an anxiety disorder at some point in our lives. These metrics make the United States the most anxious nation on the planet, according to the National Institute of Mental Health.[1]

And why wouldn't we be stressed? you might rightly ask. There is so much to worry about!

Changes in the economy and workplace have made things tough for many of us. Incomes are lower in the aggregate than they were a generation or two ago. Increasingly, contractors and part-timers do the work that used to be done by full-fledged employees—a result of the so-called gig economy. These developments are leaving many of us to scrap and scrape, to get by check to check, gig to gig.

It's not just money matters. Psychologists and sociologists say another factor is the breakdown of community in our atomized, fragmented society. We have a less robust web of relationships and support networks, a phenomenon that can be particularly acute for those who do not belong to churches or other religious communities and thus forgo their associated social benefits. In the words of the psychiatry professor Michael Davis, "If you've lost the extended family and lost the sense of community, you're going to have fewer people you can depend on, and therefore you'll be more anxious. Other cultures have much more social support and are better off psychologically because of it."[2]

I don't know about you, but when I've taken a new job I've usually had to relocate. Bye bye, friends. And, no, maintaining old friendships on Facebook, while reassuring and often enjoyable, is no substitute for the real thing.

Also fueling our anxiety is the glut of information flying at us. It's good to be well informed, but not when there is too much information of the anxiety-inducing kind. The tsunami of news and updates from our computers, smart phones, and televisions blasts our consciousness with threats, worries, conflicts, and tale after tale of people doing and saying awful things.

Property theft, identify theft, data theft. Fear of failure, fear of commitment, fear of death. The need for password security, home security, financial security, job security, national security—forms of security that we would not seek, and go to ever-greater lengths to possess, if there were not threats attached to them. Batten down the hatches, everyone! There are threats flying at us from everywhere!

Anxiety correlates with numerous bad-health behaviors and physical illnesses: smoking, alcohol and drug abuse, obesity, sleep deprivation and its associated maladies, heart disease, gastrointestinal illness, and so on. Some posit that stress and anxiety can make us more susceptible to cancer. Less dramatic but still real is the toll they can take on our work performance and our relationships with our families and friends and co-workers. Stress and anxiety can, in sum, make our lives miserable.

And some of the things we do to cope with stress only create other problems.

Has it ever occurred to you that the threats and bad possibilities are so many, so ubiquitous, that each of us could spend all day, every day, trying to identify them and protect ourselves against them? So much so that there would be no time left for anything else?

The Jesus Treatment

Back to that stressful situation we considered at the opening of the chapter: the massive crowd of people and nowhere near enough food to go around . . .

Picking up where we left off, Philip has just finished musing in Jesus's ear about the impossibility of feeding the massive crowd that has formed. Another of the disciples, Andrew, now reports the findings of the inventory. "There is a lad here who has five barley loaves and two fishes," Andrew says. "But what are they among so many?"

Not responding directly, Jesus instructs the disciples to get the people seated. He then holds the loaves, then the fishes, and expresses his gratitude for them. He starts to pass them out.

There are many religious layers to what happens next in the story—a miracle, a message for current and prospective believers about the imperative to trust in God, and so on—but as is so often the case with Jesus stories, there is meaning here, too, for those of us with a secular bent. To put that meaning in the simplest, folksiest terms, here is what comes through:

There is enough to go around. It's going to be all right.

Especially if we can expel the pesky scarcity conversation from our heads.

What the gospel writer has framed at this point in the story is the problem of "not enough." It's a problem that afflicts us today, much as it did Philip and Andrew in the story. One thing I've learned from therapy and experience is that our anxiety often grows from an assumption of scarcity. We have come to believe there is only a finite amount of opportunity and resources. We envy others for what they accomplish, believing that their success reduces our chance of being successful, too. Same goes for possessions we covet. Good things that come to someone else are hard for us to celebrate. (Now that those possessions are taken, we think, how will we ever get ours?) If someone wins a promotion or award, if someone else does something great at the office and receives the praise of the boss, it means one less open door for me. At least that's what our brains might tell us.

I'm sure you see the many ways, personal as well as professional, that this habit of mind is debilitating. We turn would-be collaborators and friends into rivals. We make it infinitely more difficult for ourselves to ever feel satisfaction with our own accomplishments. Even if we are doing very well, there are always those doing better.

When I was fortunate enough to become a regular contributor to the op-ed page of *USA Today*, other writers started approaching me for help getting a foot in the door. Without giving it any thought, I reflexively decided—maybe it was the Jesus in me—to adopt generosity as my default. I always responded with a "yes" to requests for help in opening doors. Would that mean fewer opportunities for me? Would it be smarter to hoard my access and status? Perhaps sensing the ways in which that kind of attitude had made me crazy in the past, I decided to do what I could to share the platform.

But in other contexts, scarcity still holds me in its grasp. I see how it works on me when it comes to money. It has the unfortunate effect of turning something happy into something sad. A raise, a lucrative writing gig, a gift—something to celebrate, right? Not for long. Not when scarcity takes control. I start contemplating the many possible uses for that money, the many competing needs and wants, and in a second or two I realize that the supposed windfall is much too small.

It's the same game as weekends and vacations come to an end. Do we want to waste those final precious hours we get to spend with our loved ones and favorite activities, ruing their imminent end? Or mightn't we be better off enjoying them while they last, appreciating the fact that we had them, and still *have* them, right now?

Get thee behind me, scarcity!

The trick, I'm sure you see, is to reorient our attitudes and thought processes in such a way as to perceive scarcity's opposite—abundance—and to allow ourselves to experience its fruits: gratitude and generosity. It is at this level that the loaves-and-fishes story conveys important meaning and inspiration.

More Than Enough

You have likely heard it said about global hunger that it's not a problem of there being too little food in the world or too little production capacity. There's enough food; the problem is getting it to the people who need it. Such is the dynamic at work in the place where Jesus feeds the multitudes.

I don't know what actually happened in Jesus's time (if the story has any factual basis at all). But it shows us something. With a little imagination we can see how generosity would yield abundance in that moment. Here's how:

As we discussed, the disciples' quick inventory finds a hopeless paucity of food to go around. I wager that a lot of people they surveyed were holding out for fear of not having enough for themselves. The way I see it—I, the doubting Thomas who finds the miracle story a bridge too far—some of those gathered with Jesus probably have food stashed away in their cloaks or on the premises. Or they know where to get some. They've probably been telling themselves that it's a pitifully small amount and not enough to make any difference; best to keep it for themselves so they can sneak away at some point and eat it.

Then something happens to spark the collective leap of imagination that can take us from hoarding, from scarcity, to abundance and generosity. Maybe it starts with the apparent willingness of the boy to share his loaves and fishes, meager though they are. Inspired by that, and by the stuff Jesus is teaching and preaching about compassion and generosity, someone speaks up and offers the bread she has. This inspires someone else to step forward and produce the lentils and nuts that had not existed (not officially, anyway) when he was first asked. The contagion spreads, and suddenly lots of people are pitching in. Food is "miraculously" materializing left and right. What was once a woeful scarcity becomes such an embarrassment of riches that, by story's end, everyone has eaten and the disciples are roaming the grounds and picking up twelve basketfuls of leftovers.

I can imagine Jesus winking at Philip—the stress fiend who, like me, apparently exaggerates how difficult and worrisome situations are—patting him on the shoulder, and saying, as Ron did to me back in high school, *It's going to be perfectly okay!*

Pat, pat.

"Don't Be Anxious"

The most frequently consulted passage of the Bible (at least in terms of online searches) appears in the fourth chapter of Paul's letter to the Philippians, where Paul, channeling Jesus, advises: "Do not be anxious about anything." Indeed, the Bible—the words and deeds of Jesus in particular—is a good place to look for insight, perspective, and relief in the area of stress. It's not just what Jesus is teaching but also what he is doing. The opportunity for us is not only to do what he says but to be like he was.

As my friend Wes points out, it's striking how often Jesus is removing himself from the tumult to go off alone to pray, meditate, and restore perspective. Useful practice, that—one we are well advised to implement, symbolically if not physically, the next time a stressful drama grips us in the workplace or we find ourselves locked in argument with our spouses or friends. This practice is probably a source of Jesus's consistent equanimity, and it can probably yield benefits for the rest of us, too.

It's also striking how nondefensive Jesus is. He faces authorities' criticism everywhere he goes. But rather than argue and defend himself, he invariably tells a story that at once defuses the situation and turns the showdown moment into a teaching opportunity, into a launching pad to broader, deeper understanding. Even when he is undergoing his scam trial, when he has a chance to defend himself and persuade Pilate he is unfairly accused and undeserving of arrest and execution, he leaves himself vulnerable.

Aping Jesus, I once used the opportunity presented by a new job and fresh start to adopt nondefensiveness as my default mode. In my dealings with my staff and colleagues (no, not in the job interview), I decided to be candid about mistakes and deficiencies. I discovered it worked. Some people picked up on it—one staff member marveled that she had never worked with anyone so consistently nondefensive—and appreciated my self-deprecating way of leading and relating. It made me someone they wanted to work with, and for. It drained tension from the room and encouraged others to let down their guards, too.

When we fall into our reflexive defensiveness and anxiousness, going the Jesus way can change our view and transport us to another possibility. It gets us asking useful questions of ourselves and the effect our attitude is having on ourselves, and those around us: Am I going to be one who exacerbates the anxiety in a situation by being defensive, suspicious, and prickly? Or am I going to be like Jesus and shift the dynamic toward calmness and acceptance? When it comes to stress, am I going to be part of the problem—mine and others'—or part of the solution? Am I going to pump fearfulness and anxiety into situations or, like Jesus, be a force for healing?

We can latch on to this Jesus stuff and use it even if the religious side of the story does not abide. Let's drain the anxiety from the room. For those behavior habits that are too great for us to break on our own, for those problems that are too great for us to bear alone—we can follow the simple teaching of the twelve-step meetings I used to attend. We can take those troubles and "turn them over," as my friends in the program used to say—if not to a god, then to the larger wisdom, to the collected knowledge and insight of people in our lives and people who have thought these things through, to the something-outside-our-head we might access through meditative practices. Wherever we send these worries, these plagues of anxiety, they must be cleared from the deck, taken off our plates, banished from our heads and hearts.

Turn them over, I say—and turn *to* the Jesus way, the way of equanimity that has the effect, when we commit to it, of relaxing our white-knuckle clutches and allowing us to drop the lead weights of unwarranted stress that someone has tricked us into carrying. What a relief to have our loads lightened and our hands freed.

Don't Worry?

"Therefore I tell you," Jesus is quoted as saying, "do not worry about your life, what you will eat or drink, or about your body, what you will wear. Is not life more than food and the body more than clothes? Look at the birds of the air; they do not sow or reap or store away in barns. . . . Can any one of you by worrying add a single hour to your life?"

I know a professor who takes this teaching literally and actually watches the birds flying and flittering in the woods adjacent to his house when he feels stressed. It calms him, helps put things back in perspective.

"Therefore do not worry about tomorrow," Jesus continues, "for tomorrow will worry about itself. Each day has enough trouble of its own."

Surely it can't be that simple, right? Let's pause for just a minute to examine this input. In fact, I'm going to suggest that we bring the devil's advocate into the discussion to help us sort this out.

DEVIL'S ADVOCATE: Don't worry, huh? *Seriously?* Try telling that to the cavemen we evolved from. If they didn't worry about the saber-toothed tigers or those incredibly scary bears they had back then, none of us would be here today. It's all about survival, everyone. Jesus is being naïve.

JESUS: Um, how many saber-toothed tigers did you encounter on the way to work today?

DEVIL'S ADVOCATE (TURNING TO TOM): What about Tom, our hapless author here, and the time he decided to take his then-wife (soon-to-be *ex*-wife, I might add) and small daughter to spend a few days on the North Shore of Lake Superior. It was a spur-of-the-moment thing—rather uncharacteristic of you now that I think about it, Tom. Remember that incident? "No, we won't need a reservation," you assured your soon-to-be ex. "We'll find a room at one of those little motels or cabin resorts up there, *no problem*." Never mind that the fall colors were peaking and everyone else in Minneapolis and St. Paul was also heading up there for the weekend. Tom, how much did you enjoy being turned away at inn after inn as the afternoon and then the evening wore on, and how much fun was it to drive back to St. Paul in the middle of the night with your furious soon-to-be ex?

TOM: Um, that sucked.

DEVIL'S ADVOCATE: So don't you agree it pays to worry?

TOM: Totally. It's experiences like these—and I can tick off a bunch of other examples, too—that explain why I have a hard time believing that "everything is going to be okay" despite what my old friend Ron used to say, and despite what Jesus seems to be saying. Furthermore—

JESUS (INTERRUPTING): May I say something please? You are missing my point. I am not saying you should be stupid like Tom was that time he went up to Lake Superior, when any fool could have told him all the rooms would be taken. I'm not saying the cavemen should have gone up to the saber-toothed tigers and tried to pet them. I'm not saying we shouldn't be smart and think things through. I'm talking about *worry* here, boys. And that is very different.

DEVIL'S ADVOCATE: Sounds like hairsplitting to me.

JESUS: Far from it. There's a huge difference. There's the practice of examining situations with a clear, calm head—which I strongly recommend—and then there's worry. Worry is aimless and endless. It's counterproductive. It does not add even one cubit—er, hour—to your life span or, I might add, to the quality of your life, either. Just the opposite!

Yes, I think Jesus is absolutely correct on that score. Worry is the thing. Worry is the plague we must banish—the life-sapping, joy-draining negative obsessions that get us nowhere.

Incorporating this Jesus teaching into my life does not require me to ditch good judgment and common sense. It does not compel me to make foolish decisions that are certain to cause trouble for me and those affected by my actions. It does not mean I will head out for a four-day backpacking trip without food, water, or tent. It does not mean that when the inspiration hits me to become a musician, a songwriter, a poet, I will abruptly quit my job to pursue my new passion despite the fact that I have a kid to feed. It does not mean I can abdicate my responsibility as a caring citizen to pay attention to what's happening in our world and try to have a constructive influence. It does not mean that we can blithely ignore our responsibility to preserve for future generations, for today's kids and their kids and *their* kids, a society and a planet that are conducive to their having decent, healthy lives.

We are talking about *worry* here, folks—that pernicious plague of the mind that makes us turn molehills into mountains, that lures us into treating imagined worst-case scenarios as objective realities and into experiencing them, having emotional responses to them, as if they are real—all at a high, high cost to our ability to sleep, to think clearly, and to enjoy any peace of mind. Jesus is not teaching us to forgo complex, responsible thinking but advising us to abandon *worry*—the habit that can make our lives miserable while accomplishing absolutely nothing.

Worry, the Christian author Amy Simpson writes, is something that "humans do with simple fear once it reaches the part of their brain called the cerebral cortex. We make fear complex, adding anticipation, memory, imagination, and emotion. Worry is not a helpful activity that moves us forward; it's a repetitive cycle that keeps us stuck."[3]

As my pastor friend Matthew Croasmun writes, "Jesus is all about living in the moment for the sake of what lasts forever. Everything else—all the tomorrows to come—are a 'no man's land' in which we're bound to get lost in worry."[4]

I know people who turn worry into a virtue, a sign of how much they care. They tempt you to go there, too. Maybe it's because misery loves company. I'm saying this to myself now as much as to you: Don't go!

A Most Welcome Futility

Has it ever occurred to you that, ultimately, it's all out of our hands? That no matter how much security we attempt to build, buy, and borrow, no one, over the many millennia and over the spans of gazillions upon gazillions of human lifetimes, has yet figured out how to stay alive for more than a few score decades?

And that accepting this is kind of a relief?

The psychologists tell us that a lack of control over our life circumstances, having no agency in what happens to us day to day, correlates with stress and anxiety. That's true; powerlessness *is* a debilitating curse, and I do not wish it upon anyone (except those who would abuse their power to hurt others). But we have to recognize the borderline where we stop having any legitimate pretense to control, where hoarding it is a self-deceiving and self-defeating game, where our desperate attempts to do the impossible—stay forever young, protect ourselves against every imaginable hurt or vulnerability, manage what every person in our sphere is feeling and doing—make us behave strangely. *The illusion of control.* For me, it conjures the picture of a man hoarding a small pool of water in his cupped hands. I'm sure you see how little he is going to be able to do as long as he holds on to the water that way—and how freeing it will be for him when he finally lets that water go or, better yet, slurps it up.

I am convinced we should take a cue from Jesus—the Jesus who slept, actually *slept*, through the fury of a squall that rocked the boat on which he and the disciples were traveling one day. Predictably, the combination of the storm and

Jesus's apparent lack of concern causes the disciples to freak out, which seems to have been something of a pattern with them, as with me. How instructive that the disciples actually criticized Jesus for his equanimity, as if worry were a virtue. "Don't you care if we drown?" they asked him.

Typical Jesus—he doesn't get defensive, here or anywhere else, as far as I can tell. He just calms the storm—the actual storm that's tossing the boat, if you believe it that way, and the storm that's howling in the disciples' hearts.

The Jesus teachings, the Jesus example, encourage us to do something extremely important and conducive to mental health. Jesus is urging us, namely, to stop sweating the small stuff, to keep things in perspective. Jesus is urging us to keep our eyes on the prize, the big picture, the long view, the things that really matter and always endure whatever today's circumstances might bring.

How easily the trees block our view of the forest. It happened with Jesus's critics, those who scoffed at something wonderful and compassionate he was doing in one Bible scene (healing people) because of a technicality having to do with the day of the week (Mark 3:1–6). Healing people on the *Sabbath*? Heaven forfend!

I doubt those being healed had much of a problem with what day it was.

Take a cue from Jesus and accept the comfort of the big-picture things that last beyond this week's dramas. What's better? Gnashing your teeth about real and imagined shortages within earshot of your spouse or kid, or telling them you love them? Stewing about your colleague's promotion (why not you?) or being happy for her or him and appreciating the job and pay that you do have, which are so much more than those possessed by most people on the planet? What's better? Fretting about what might happen tomorrow or experiencing and savoring the good thing happening *right now*?

When she takes her cue from Jesus, Amy Simpson, for one, finds herself better able to keep worry at bay. "I check my attitude toward the future," she explains. "Am I trying to see something I don't have the ability to see? I check my attitude toward possessions and people: Am I trying to hang on to something that really isn't mine? I try to pull back to a bigger-picture perspective: How important is this really?"[5]

Often, that on which we are fixating is *not* especially important, we discover, and not at all worthy of the "price" we are paying for it.

Jesus was not a psychiatrist. But the way he's portrayed in the Bible, he seems to be absolutely enlightened about stress and worry, completely unburdened by them, and keen to share his insight with anyone who will listen.[6] Even the practices he taught that are not explicitly about stress contribute to our having less stressed lives. Things like: Don't envy. Don't hate. Don't fear.

"Come to me," he says, "all you who are weary and carrying heavy burdens, and I will give you rest."

I'm on my way.

Chapter Five

SAVED FROM *WHAT?*

You deserve it.

You've heard that one before, haven't you?

If not from the ubiquitous advertisements, maybe you've had it put to you by the voice in your head—the one that preys on thoughts about how hard you have it and how little appreciation you get. Those stylish new shoes and that impressive new suit you've been thinking about really *are* owed to you (credit card balances be damned). You put up with so much. You work so hard. It's been *so* long since you've treated yourself and enjoyed that little dopamine jolt you receive from finding and *getting* something you really want.

That voice in my head used to purr about things like slick watches and cool-looking track jackets with soccer team logos. More often these days, it tries to get me with promises of a break from my labors, from demands on my oh-so-precious time. When the alarm goes off at 5:40 A.M. and it's time to write before I go to my regular work, that voice—call him Petulant Tom—starts right in: *Dude, you should take it a bit easier. Sleep in a little! What the hell were you thinking when you committed yourself to the death sentence of starting another book?* (Yes, Petulant Tom lapses into serious hyperbole at times.) *Really? You've done enough. You have it* so *hard. Take the morning off. You deserve it!*

Does life boil down to nothing more than noticing our needs and desires and trying to gratify them? I'm hungry; I will seek and consume food. I'm tired; I will rest. The thing I am doing now has me feeling restless and bored; I will do something else. My clothing options are too few and not quite right; I will hit up Banana Republic for some new shirts and trousers.

On virtually the same day I was writing this paragraph, into my e-mail in-box came an enthusiastic notice from Banana Republic that the online store had some incredible new stuff I should buy. Why? "Because," the subject line said, "you deserve it." The next time I have the proposition put to me in one of these e-mail pitches, I swear I will send back a reply with the subject line: "No, I don't deserve it." And in the body of the e-mail I will point out that I have had enough of these endless unsupported appeals to my selfishness. "Who says I deserve this," I will say, "and why must you keep trying to slip that pernicious thought into my head?"

Other than dignity and human rights, what do any of us deserve, really?

Mine has been a struggle to steer my train of thought to more edifying tracks. When I get in touch with gratitude, when I get in touch with patience, when I get in touch with generosity, when I get in touch with the empathy I have for the billions of people who have it way worse than I do, when I get in touch with the fact that the universe does not exist to meet my preferences and desires, when I get in touch with something bigger—when I get in touch with Jesus—the Petulant Tom voice struggles for a hearing. The "I need" conversation, the "I want" conversation, the "I resent" conversation recedes to a more distant province of my thoughts and feelings. I become more quietly content and able to grasp that there are lots and lots of other people in my sphere and on this planet, too.

How are *they* doing? What are *they* going through?

That, I hope you see, is what starts to change everything.

Jesus Saves?

The "Jesus saves" message on offer from Christianity has always left me a little cold. *Are you saved?* This has been the faith's central question in our time, at least in Christianity's more conservative circles. Even if it's not stated explicitly, most of us, whether we are Christian or otherwise, know the proposition: Accept Jesus as your personal lord and savior or face an afterlife of eternal torment and punishment.

It's a shame that Jesus is set up this way. It has the unfortunate effect of making him irrelevant to the many of us who will not or cannot buy into the whole heaven and hell thing. And it erases the enormously rich set of Jesus teachings and insights relevant to *this* world, *this* life. For those of us who are unmoved by the otherworldly promise attached to Jesus, it's worth considering what else he might bring.

Jesus saves, you say? From *what*?

At a church service I crashed in downtown Portland once, I heard a young, hip pastor named John Mark Comer address this "Jesus saves" notion for a church full of mostly high school– and college-age people. No doubt aware that evangelicalism's up-and-comers don't greatly resonate with the notion of faith based on hell avoidance, this preacher explored a different way to conceive of that ubiquitous phrase and promise: *Jesus saves.*

Jesus, he explained, saves you from a life devoted to the wrong things. Jesus saves you from living a meaningless life. Jesus saves you from a life that misses the point.

This is something about Jesus I can grab on to. When I hear this, the idealist in me vibrates in assent. Who wants to spend her or his whole life chasing after desires that don't satisfy? Who wants to realize on her deathbed that she has missed the point of life and has no chance to do it over? If there's a hell, that, to me, is it.

Seeking Satisfaction in All the Wrong Places

For some human beings, wealth is the lodestar. Accumulating and enjoying material riches is the point of life. For some, it's power. For others—here's my category—it's external validation, success, status. Does my job title impress? Do my articles appear in the largest-circulation media outlets? Do I have enough awards and Twitter followers to justify my existence? Back in my undergraduate years, when getting A's was central to my having a positive view of myself, I remember thinking about good grades the way an addict regards his drugs or alcohol. At the end of a semester once, as I strode across campus to the professor's office to get my grade, I remember saying to myself: *This better be an A. I need this fix.*

It's not that I consciously chose this orientation, this addiction. It just came to be.

"Forces bigger than ourselves—perhaps most of all, marketing and pop culture—shape our goals without us realizing it, guiding our lives for us, often in directions that, were we to think about it, we would want to resist." This insight comes courtesy of an article cowritten by Miroslav Volf, a theology professor at Yale Divinity School whose work explores big questions like What is the point of life? What is a life worth living? Volf and his coauthor, Ryan McAnnally-Linz, go on to note: "Life becomes, for instance, a series of consumer decisions based on our preferences for this or that experience, or a mad race for some vaguely defined 'success.'"[1]

Ours is an age when we are free to pursue what makes us happy. So we are told. But think about it carefully, observe your behavior for a moment, and you might see this: Our desires often control *us*, and they are not necessarily the desires we would independently choose if we sat down with ourselves for a serious talk. *This* is freedom?

While you're pondering that, consider this, too: When are we ever satisfied? When it comes to possessions, thrilling experiences, and status, when do we have *enough*?

Enough is tricky. The definition seems to keep changing. It's like you're a quarterback driving your football team down the field, getting first down after first down, advancing into the red zone, and just when you think you've reached the goal line, the officials magically push the line back twenty or thirty yards. You keep driving, you keep pushing, and each time you think you've reached the goal line called "enough," the definition of the concept shifts, and what you have now is most definitely *not* enough.

"No matter how high you go in life and no matter how many accolades you win, it's never enough," writes *New York Times* columnist David Brooks, a man who has achieved a level of journalistic status and success matched by few. "The desire for even more admiration races ahead. Career success never really satisfies. Public love always leaves you hungry. Even very famous people can do self-destructive things in an attempt to seem just a little cooler."[2]

Counting on career and economic success to fulfill us, Brooks writes in a different piece, is "the central illusion of our time."[3]

Competing for top spot on that list is the illusion that consuming goods and services can fulfill us. Like status and success, consumerism sings a compelling siren song—and ultimately deceives. The thrill we get from scoring a new tablet, the latest iPhone, that sixty-inch flat-screen, high-def television, is fleeting. If you like to buy jerseys of pro soccer teams (a weakness of mine), you learn that the system is rigged to make the shirts obsolete within a year or two; teams change their designs virtually every year. What's impressive today can leave you feeling like a dork in a season or two.

When you think you're finally getting to the point where you have everything you need, you discover an embarrassing lack that you had previously overlooked. Bad news! Advertisers are great at pointing this out to you. But rest assured, they have just the product or service you need to solve this newfound problem.

The teeth-whitening promoters got in my head that way. I had been cruising along for years not worrying about the shade of my teeth before the advertisers finally snared me. Suddenly I felt naïve and stupid. I realized my smile wasn't bright enough. Imagine the cruel judgments people had been making about me all along! I bought the damn whitening strips. And thus was I saved. Until the next problem came along.

Among the West Coast foodies and sustainability devotees with whom I consorted in my Portland days, I found an obsessiveness about food choices, food ethics, and food politics that made me wonder if this preoccupation had taken on the status of a kind of secular "salvation." The Christian author and food activist Sara Miles thinks so. "Sometimes I think I'll scream if I hear anyone say 'organic' or 'local' or 'artisan' not to mention 'single source' or 'farm to table' again," the San Francisco–based Miles writes. "Does buying all-organic groceries make you a better person? Can Kale *save*?"[4]

You can guess Miles's answer: No. What *can* save, she posits, is the radical fellowship she sees in the Jesus story, the act of "sitting down and eating with others—especially with strangers and the impure, as Jesus does."

Some of the other sources to which progressive seculars turn likewise prove wanting on closer examination, in more honest moments. We love our music, art, progressive politics, sustainability, bicycling culture, separately and in combination, and we experience much that is good, even beautiful. Some people turn to yoga, some to running, some to nature, some to climbing. There is good in all of these. But do they have enough size and heft to give a life *meaning*?

A Different Kind of Wealth

What is fascinating about the Jesus story—what makes it so irresistibly applicable to our unsatisfying pursuits of satisfaction—is the utter lack of material wealth, power, and status he amassed during his thirty-some years on the planet. In the pantheon of towering figures in history, you will be hard-pressed to find any who can match him in that regard. Of course there are many great political and religious figures who endured hardship and scorn, whose sufferings played a role in their achievements on behalf of their fellow humans. But no one else of his stature suffered a cross. It's puzzling, when you think about it, that a religion revolving around an outcast "loser" has loomed so large in an American culture that places tremendous value on material success and never-ending economic growth. Sure, rising from the dead might qualify as the ultimate impressive accomplishment, and some Christians place their eggs in this basket, spending little time dwelling on the aspects of Jesus's career that our culture would judge failures. But when it comes to material, earthly accomplishments, the Jesus résumé does not impress. Status? For the climactic chapter of his life, he rode into town on a dumpy donkey!

Yet that donkey, the direction in which Jesus was riding it, the mission he was on—all these point to an approach to life that actually can save us from so much of what ails.

I dwelt on these matters one year in the run-up to Christmas. It was 2009, the country was in the depths of the Great Recession, and I was working on a column about what the headline would term "the real gifts of Christmas." The recession, I suggested, presented a prime opportunity for us to question the conceits of consumerism and the rarely examined imperative for material acquisition. Many of us, more than usual, could not afford to splurge at Christmastime in the customary fashion that year.

Perfect, I said. We were wanting the wrong things anyway. What mattered most, I suggested, were the "possessions" we could not earn through our strivings, the treasures that transcend our ownership and yet can never be taken away from us: The love and kindness of our friends and families and spouses. The mountains and oceans. Music and poetry. The sun rising each day. The fact of existence—our own and that of the vast mysterious universe. The knowledge, if we can work ourselves up to it, that each of us is inherently valuable regardless of what the culture says with its shallow, status-obsessed, me-me-me messages.

For the sun and the dawn which we did not create;
. . . We lift up our hearts in thanks.

The sentiment of this poem (Richard Fewkes, "We Lift Up Our Hearts") is not what the purveyors of consumerism want us to internalize. It takes the edge off our materialistic strivings. It has the dangerous potential to make us feel grateful and satisfied. It lures us to a conception of life where we begin to actually get what it's all about.

This poem is one source of inspiration and insight on these matters. So are the teachings attributed to Jesus in his Sermon on the Mount. Among its other valuable takeaways, it challenges the strivers and consumers like me to refocus on sources of sustenance that actually *can* satisfy, and to a kind of living that indeed can save us from pointlessness.

> Do not store up for yourselves treasures on earth, where moths and vermin destroy, and where thieves break in and steal. But store up for yourselves treasures in heaven, where moths and vermin do not destroy, and where thieves do not break in and steal. For where your treasure is, there your heart will be also.

Whether we take "heaven" literally or figuratively, Jesus is challenging us to focus on ends more edifying than becoming important and wealthy by society's standards. Power, status, riches—Jesus had them all if he wanted them. In the Bible telling, Satan offers these to Jesus. Consider the devil a stand-in for the forces in culture that dangle these temptations in our sight, in New Testament times as today. Jesus said no. It has often occurred to me that the Jesus of the Bible who has the power to walk on water and turn water into wine could probably have scored any possession or political victory he wanted. His rejecting these prizes for a nobler path—one of sacrifice for others—is loaded with moral truth.

Earthly treasures are ephemeral. A misstep or two, a turn of bad luck, the arrival of devastating circumstances beyond our control, and—boom—they are gone. Reversals of fortunate circumstance, our tendency to grow dissatisfied with what we have—these are among the "moths and vermin" that threaten our earthly stores. What are we left with after they finish their marauding? Even if we are not vexed by odious turns for the worse, even if we do not lose our lofty titles, our sterling reputations, and our well-appointed homes, our earthly treasures have a nasty habit of changing right before our eyes. What was enough yesterday may leave us in want today. It's as if treasures shrink, even though their dimensions remain exactly the same. We think we need more, then more again.

Dissatisfaction is rampant in American culture. Consider how central our jobs are to our lives. They dominate our time. They afford us food and shelter and, if we are lucky, a measure of enjoyment, pride, and comradeship with our co-workers. Yet our jobs are sources of dissatisfaction for most—70 percent of us, according to one survey.[5] Other polls find us dissatisfied with government, dissatisfied with our laws, dissatisfied with immigration levels, dissatisfied with the health-care system, dissatisfied with the education system, and dissatisfied with the direction of the country. We have conveniences and comforts and entertainments and technologies that would dazzle the generations who came before us, and we are . . . dissatisfied. Happiness—the pursuit of which is enshrined in the country's founding document, the experience of which we spend so much time chasing—eludes us.

In "Unsatisfied," a great indie rock song from the 1980s, Paul Westerberg, songwriter and singer for the Replacements, articulates the experience for many of us, certainly for me. Noting that he has everything he ever wanted, yet still senses something is wrong, he howls a lyric as blunt as it is perceptive: "I'm so, I'm so, unsatisfied!"

This is one reason why Jesus remains so relevant. He models an engagement with life radically different from the one we so easily slip into. His teachings seem to have anticipated the obsessions of our time, and offer us the way out we so dearly need.

Consider, for example, material salvation.

If things are going badly for me lately, if my material circumstances do not constitute the American Dream, if I am not contributing much to the gross domestic product, the barrage of messages from the culture will tell me I am worthless. If I *am* doing well, the ethos of the culture afflicts me with something equally damaging to society's and my well-being. All those others who are struggling? I am mightily tempted to judge them as failures, the causes of their own misery. Thus, I have the pretense I need to wash my hands of them.

The humanizer par excellence, the giver in chief, Jesus teaches that I am *not* worthless, whatever the culture might say. Not under any circumstances. And the corollary: Jesus shows you that you cannot so haughtily condemn and walk away from those around you who suffer. Yes, that could be you. Equally important, loving that neighbor changes *you* for the better. Imagine how our lives would be transformed, individually and collectively, if we always treated the low the same way we treat the high.

As I wrote in that Christmastime column in 2009, challenging myself as much as the readers of *USA Today,* there is something uplifting in training our sights not on what we might buy or otherwise *get* but on the unearned gifts that Richard Fewkes talks about in his poetic words about gratitude. Let's draw inspiration, I wrote, from the "savior" celebrated at Christmas who showed that we *all* have value, whatever our "net worth." Committing to this conception of life more than to material things, more than to self-seeking and self-gratification, is the way to lasting satisfaction and something approaching fulfillment.

Don't hold your breath waiting for the advertisers to say it. But this is the one thing in our "you-deserve-it" culture that each of us actually *does* deserve, and that each of us can count on. You might call it our humanity.

The Anthem of the Age

A lot of us, I fear, exaggerate our nearness to the center of the universe. Tune your ears to what the culture is saying and you start hearing the message that it's all about you. As naturally follows, losing yourself is one of the worst fates that can befall you. The principal goal in life? *Finding* yourself. Being *true* to yourself. Peeling back the layers of deception, the agendas imposed by others, to identify what will bring you fulfillment. Making that authentic *you* the object of your pursuits.

There's a magazine with a title that says it all about our self-seeking lives. It's called, simply, *Self.* And who could forget the *Time* magazine cover from 2013 showing a young woman taking a selfie photo under a headline blaring, THE ME, ME, ME GENERATION? The accompanying story was an exaggerated and rather unfair critique of the millennial generation. Couldn't all our generations be similarly indicted?

Truly, "me, me, me," if put to music, would be an accurate anthem for our era. Yet the enduring popularity of another song with a seemingly different message complicates the sound track, hinting at a dissatisfaction with all-out pursuit of ourselves. It's that countermessage telling you to get *out* of your head, to get *out* of yourself. In the sway of this message, we seek to *lose* ourselves in some amazing experience, in wondrous moments when we "become one" with nature, our lovers, the universe. The increasingly popular promoters of meditation extol the sublime experience of losing our separateness, our overwhelming awareness of self—being free from what Sam Harris calls the thinkers we all seem to have in our brains, constituting what it means to be "you."

I, for one, can comprehend the attractiveness of this notion. My head is a place full of low-grade anxiety, trivial grievances, constant self-questioning, and ever-present wondering about where I stand with others. It's no place you would want to stay for very long.

I used to be an ardent pickup basketball player. When I thought about why I loved the game so much, I realized the key was that I found it utterly absorbing. Thinking about where to run, what opening I might find to fire off a shot, who was open for a pass, the position of my defender, the movements of the guy I was guarding, who was about to step out and set a pick on me—all this rapid mental (not to mention physical) exertion left not a scintilla of space in my brain for the stuff that usually afflicts a self-conscious person like me. I lost myself in the experience.

Same with mountain climbing, a sport I picked up in middle age. Where to plant your ice ax, where to kick your next step into the hard snow, where to find the next handhold and foothold on the rock face? These concerns focus the mind, especially when a slipup could send you careening down a steep, icy mountainside until you crash into rocks or trees—or over a cliff. An experience like this will get you "out of your head" for sure.

What do all the alcohol and drugs consumed in our culture suggest if not desperation to *escape* our bored, hurting, unsatisfactory selves?

So which is it? Is the point to find ourselves, or to lose ourselves?

My guess is that we mostly fall for the former. When we engage the latter, we do so in a spirit of escapism, and in pursuit of that ever-present end called "personal gratification." Yet there is something in that fleeting but persistent desire to lose ourselves that deserves attention. It seems to suggest that we find something mundane and unsatisfactory about that "me, me, me" song, that we long for something more.

Enter Charles Taylor. If you believe what this venerable Canadian philosopher writes in his magisterial book *A Secular Age*, something *does* pull at us—a vague, nagging sense that something is missing from a conception of life that is purely material, largely self-oriented, and utterly closed off to any possibility of transcendence. Taylor likens this feeling to a "ghost" from centuries past when our more religious ancestors perceived supernatural agency virtually everywhere. We are "haunted," Taylor posits, by the feeling that there could be, should be, more than our material world. It can plague us with ennui, jadedness, the state of being perpetually "unsatisfied" that the Replacements articulated with such ragged urgency. Writes James K. A. Smith in his examinations of Taylor's work: "There is a specter haunting our secular age, 'the spectre of meaninglessness.' "[6]

Taylor himself writes, "Some people sense a terrible flatness in the everyday. . . . They feel the emptiness of the repeated, accelerating cycle of desire and fulfillment in consumer culture; the cardboard quality of bright supermarkets, or neat row housing in a clean suburb."[7]

Taylor's insights ring true. I suspect we could add many bullet points to the list of objectives that leave us feeling "flat" if or when we achieve them: success at our careers, success at gaining financial security, success at living the experiences on our "bucket lists."

Yet as Taylor acknowledges, there is no returning to the thoroughly religious age that preceded our secular time; nonbelief is now an option in everyone's face, and that genie is not going back in the bottle anytime soon. It is unlikely that most of us secular people will discover or rediscover religious faith before our time is up. Without belief in the supernatural, without acceptance of "God" as traditionally conceived, how can we, the nonreligious, experience the fullness that many of us might miss? How can we follow this impulse toward something more lasting and edifying than a product or a thrill?

What *can* fulfill?

Far be it from me to offer any pretentious final answers. But I will point in a general direction, the direction in which I find Jesus pointing me. It's the direction away from myself and toward something "other." Toward other *people*, to be precise—toward empathy and generosity. This, I am convinced, is a way toward that nebulous prize we might call greater meaning and fulfillment.

Play That Other Song

In his ageless Sermon on the Mount, Jesus advises us to be careful about how we evaluate and dismiss others. "Do not judge, or you too will be judged," he says. The way the sermon is rendered in Luke's gospel, Jesus takes this train of thought a station or two further: "Do not condemn, and you will not be condemned," he says. "Forgive, and you will be forgiven."

Does it always work out this way? If you change your attitude about the nasty supervisor or co-worker who is vexing you, will it naturally play out that he or she will suddenly start treating you better? If you and a loved one have been cruel to one another, will your forgiveness of him or her assure that you will be forgiven in turn? No on both counts. But this shift in attitude evoked by Jesus can change our experience of painful turns in our relationships. It can alter our relationship to them and other vexing situations, which can lead to productive breakthroughs in how we navigate them. Sometimes, in the best-case scenarios, this shift might even inspire a positive turn in the behavior of those with whom we are in conflict. If more of us started incorporating this Jesus practice into our day-to-day interactions, the dynamics could shift, couldn't they?

"Why do you look at the speck of sawdust in your brother's eye," Jesus goes on to ask, "and pay no attention to the plank in your own eye? You hypocrite, first take the plank out of your eye, and then you will see clearly to remove the speck from your brother's eye."

When it's time to condemn and punish, Jesus says, let the

one who is perfect initiate the proceedings. I think we can all see how seldom condemnations and punishments will commence if this is our approach.

These insights of Jesus grab me by the lapels. I find them messing with our twenty-first-century minds in just the right ways. What a counterforce they pose to our narcissistic tendencies. How often have you observed people complaining endlessly about the mistreatment they are suffering from people in their lives, about the horrible behavior and callous deeds inflicted on them by others, while they remain oblivious to the harm they dispense, to the possibility that someone at that very moment could be laying out, quite justifiably, a similar case against them? Maybe while I'm looking in the mirror to remove the plank in my eye, I will catch a glimpse of the ways in which I am the cause of others' suffering. Maybe I will see that those whom I condemn are not all that different from the guy in the mirror.

Jesus also speaks of love in this sermon, the hardest kind of love we can imagine: that which we have for our "enemies." As he put it:

> If you love those who love you, what credit is that to you? Even sinners love those who love them. And if you do good to those who are good to you, what credit is that to you? Even sinners do that. And if you lend to those from whom you expect repayment, what credit is that to you?

Jesus is making an important distinction between transactional "love" and the kind of love—the unconditional kind—that is given with no expectation of repayment or interest. Seriously, even your bank can show you "love" of the first sort.

What Jesus summons is a kind of love that revolves around no self-seeking motive, no quid pro quo. If I do something "generous" for you but make it plainly evident that "you owe me one," that is not exactly generosity, is it? If you buy your new girlfriend a beautiful necklace and take her to an elegant dinner while feeling entitled to awesome sex for dessert, that is not exactly "love." That's putting something out with an expectation that someone will be putting out for you. It's not altogether different from the motive of the bank in "giving" me money to buy a house. It's business.

Jesus is talking about a no-strings-attached giving of oneself. It's a gift, not a deal. And it's hard. Virtually nothing in culture encourages us to behave this way.

"To you who are listening," Jesus preaches, "I say: Love your enemies, do good to those who hate you. Bless those who curse you, pray for those who mistreat you."

Yeah, right. Who's going to actually do that?

Jesus did it in his death throes, according to the Bible account. He asked for forgiveness for the soldiers who were carrying out his execution, famously and accurately noting that they did not know what the hell they were doing.

This radical generosity of spirit is nearly impossible to implement. It's hard even for traditional believers, and they have the extra incentive of an eternal reward. What could possibly motivate the rest of us to follow this Jesus teaching, if only a little?

If it's an ontological answer you seek, there's this: It is the right thing to do—the right thing of the highest order. (Who says secular people cannot make unsupported philosophical pronouncements about ultimate right and wrong?)

If you prefer something a little less philosophical, try this: Generosity of this sort can start to change the world. If it were to begin catching on—and who says it can't?—it would make the environments in which we live more like the places we would want to spend our limited time. It would be conducive to a state of affairs in which we not only treat others this way but receive this treatment ourselves.

There is a way of seeing this impossible imperative that makes it not only helpful but eminently "doable" for those who are not ready to sacrifice ourselves to the boss who is persecuting us or the ex-spouse who is antagonizing us. What if we silently acknowledged that they, like the guards who carried out Jesus's execution, knew not what they were doing? What if we recognized the larger forces and pressures that were antagonizing and manipulating them, and we mustered a thimbleful of compassion? What if we spent a minute examining ourselves and thinking about the possibility that we are the instruments of misery in someone else's life?

Would this practice instantly transform the world? No. But it can start to change our experience of it. And it can start to change how we treat others, and how they, in turn, treat us. Who knows where it can lead?

An Anchor Worthy of Trust

Here is how Jesus-style love is described by Paul, one of his first major interpreters and promoters. Love, Paul writes in his first letter to the Jesus followers at Corinth, is patient. It is kind. It does not envy or boast. It keeps no record of wrongs. It is not self-seeking. And—key part here—it never fails.

Love that never fails?

As my theologian friend Matthew Croasmun reminds me, Paul is talking about fail-proof love in a religious sense, as something that endures for eternity, after our bodies and world are long gone. Religious though it may be, there is something in the concept that we secular folks can grab on to as well.

Love that never fails: It calls to mind the importance of anchors in mountain climbing, as we considered in the opening of this book, the need for an immovable boulder or deeply rooted tree to which the climb team can attach the fixed line, and to which each climber can commit his or her safety—his or her *life*—while negotiating a steep, dangerous pitch.

It's my wager that if we pick our anchors well and commit to them, if we live into them and live them out, something like a self-fulfilling prophecy can happen. Our lives can take on new clarity and depth, and begin to attain something approaching the "fullness" of which the philosopher Charles Taylor speaks.

Mine is an ongoing process of deciding to climb. The radical love in the Jesus story is the direction in which I'm going. And it's the rock of Jesus's ethics and way of living to which I am anchoring my line.

Whether I have chosen that anchor well depends, I suppose, on what I ultimately want. If it's comfort, possessions, invulnerability, and status, I will need to find a different anchor or, more likely, not climb at all. But if it's a life oriented toward something more than self-seeking and "what's in it for me?" calculating, I trust that line is going to hold.

Jesus saves? He *can*, actually, depending on what you mean. I have come to see that following Jesus can save us from a life of trivial pursuits, from a life lived in vain, from a life that misses the point. Following Jesus, I suggest, can save us from a life limited to that small and tiresome world revolving around "me" and that which the almighty *I* can acquire.

Following Jesus, I suggest, can save us from a life wasted on living only for ourselves.

Chapter Six

SECULAR IN THE CITY

When I lived in Portland, one of the most pleasant cities in the country, teeming with some of the most cheerful city dwellers you will ever encounter, I started listening a little too much to the misanthrope in my head. In the district where my wife and I lived, the charming coffeehouses and bars and restaurants and shops and galleries drew people like bugs to a light. On foot, on bikes, in cars, people everywhere. Getting in one another's way. Getting in *my* way.

Pedestrians rule in Portland—at least they are supposed to. Asserting your rights and stepping out into the crosswalk becomes a nervy adventure when an impatient driver is bearing down. *Is he going to stop, for God's sake?* The situation my wife and I came to "love" even more: a vehicle blocking the crosswalk. Especially when it was a massive SUV.

Funny how my view of pedestrians would change when I was the impatient one behind the wheel. Picture the scene: I am inching up Glisan Street, thwarted by one red light after another. I finally reach Fourteenth Avenue, where I can make the right-hand turn and drive those last few blocks to the comfort of home. I'm ready to pull out and . . . hold on. Suddenly there's a mass of walkers crossing the street and blocking the path. Isn't there always? Of course, one of those pedestrians is emulating a snail now, crawling across . . . at . . . the . . . slowest . . . pace . . . ever . . . recorded . . . in . . . the . . . annals . . . of . . . human . . . motion. The slow guy is almost out of the way when the distracted person standing on the corner staring into her iPhone decides that she is now going to cross, too. Ack! Waiting, waiting, waiting. The light turns red, and stuck I remain. An unbroken line of cars zip past, left to right, crushing any hope of my making the turn I so dearly want to make. I inch ahead and crane my neck for a clearer view. Damn—no openings. I am stranded in a dicey spot now, obstructing the crosswalk and bearing repeated stabbings by the pedestrians' dagger stares. *Don't they understand my predicament?*

I reach a point—perhaps you do, too, if you spend time in a crowded urban setting—where the misanthrope inside takes over. *People, get out of my way. You're annoying the hell out of me!*

How seldom it occurs to me that *I* am in *their* way.

People stop being people. They become objects that get in the way. Living in the crowded city can get you thinking like this.

But seeing these annoying objects as Jesus did can turn them back into people.

Our Urban Age

Cities, the places where people are found in especially large numbers, are where our humanity is hardest to see, and honor.

"Sociability seems to bear an inverse relationship to the density of the population," writes Alain de Botton in his insightful *Religion for Atheists.* "We generally talk gladly to people only once we have also the option of avoiding them altogether." People in urban centers, de Botton adds, "must—in order to preserve a modicum of inner serenity—give no sign of even noticing the millions of humans who are eating, sleeping, arguing, copulating, and dying only centimeters away from them on all sides."[1]

It's true: We don't have the time as we race down the street, on our way to work or a meeting or a social engagement with a human we actually know. How would we have the bandwidth to approach the person slumped on the curb alone, head in hands, spilling tears, or the rags-clad man out cold in the middle of the sidewalk, drunk or dead, we don't know, to find out what's wrong and how we might help?

Were we to investigate these scenes each time we encountered them, we would probably never make it to where we are going and probably never do the things we need, and want, to do. If we got involved with each suffering person we came across out there on the streets, we would no doubt subject ourselves to hassles and complications and strains on our budgets (maybe even threats to our physical safety) that we would come to regret. As de Botton suggests, were we to deeply *feel* something about the misery in our faces and under our feet each time we ventured out in the city, our lives would be unmanageable, brought down by too much . . . compassion. We steel ourselves, not because we are inherently cold and unfeeling, but because we must if we are to get through the day. And it's not like those of us who are "making it" are experiencing each day as a cakewalk.

These dynamics have been present as long as people have been congregating in large communities. But their relevance, their poignancy, are greater now than ever. Ours is an urban age. More than any time in human history, we work, play, live, and die in cities. Cities in the United States, although they occupy a mere 3 percent of the country's land space, generate 90 percent of the country's gross domestic product and 86 percent of the jobs.[2] More than 80 percent of us in the United States reside in urban areas. Cities, by and large, are where the art is being created, businesses are being hatched, and exciting new ideas are germinating. A century ago, just 15 percent of the world's population were city dwellers. In 1990, urban areas still claimed less than 40 percent of the world's population. The World Health Organization reports that now, for the first time ever, the majority of people live in cities.[3] This is a majority projected to grow ever larger—to the point where some 70 percent of the earth's inhabitants will live in cities by the middle of this century.

The urban experience is, increasingly, the *human* experience, complete with its many aspects that could be best described as dehumanizing.

Jesus often seems nowhere in sight in the cities, which in addition to being the places where all the action happens, are the places where our culture's secularizing trend is most pronounced. Portland's Pearl District, which is where my wife and I lived, has nary a church building. Setting aside the orthodox religious assertions about Jesus—his status as the divine son of God, his ability to save us from our sins if we accept him as savior—and taking a clear-eyed look at life in the secular city, we might arrive at an astonishing realization:

We could really use some Jesus in the secular city. Especially the stuff Jesus taught, and demonstrated, about the imperative to accept the worth of every human being and care about him or her no matter how offensive, annoying, ugly, poorly dressed, old, smelly, racially or culturally different, or just plain uncool that person might appear.

Out of Network

One day, a man asks Jesus to elaborate on the well-known religious imperative to "love your neighbor as yourself." Who, this interlocutor asks, *is* our neighbor? Jesus, as usual, tells a story. This is how it goes:

A man is lying by the side of Jericho Road. He's been the victim of an assault, we learn. He is beaten up, in obvious distress—"half dead," as it's phrased in the New International Version of the Bible.

Two men are walking down this same road and reach the spot where our victim lies in misery. They are, Jesus points out, respectable members of the Jewish community with elevated religious status, one a priest, the other a "Levite." Surely, they will stop and tend to the beat-up crime victim, right?

I'm afraid not. No doubt hurrying to an important

meeting or task, the two men do what I might do were I a character in the story. They walk on by. We can only hope that if cell phones had existed in those days, the priest and the Levite would have had the decency to call 911 and report what they had seen. But to stop and care for the man? Who of us would have time? Who would be ready to take on *that* drama? Isn't that for the police, or some service agency, or someone less busy to handle? So it goes in our hectic days.

It's the next part of Jesus's story that really sticks. We learn that a third passerby is coming. Maybe there's hope, after all. Or maybe not. We find out he's a Samaritan. Living in our time and place, we often hear about or refer to a helpful person as a "Good Samaritan." The term has warm associations. Not so for the Jewish community to whom Jesus is speaking when he tells the story. *Lowlifes, outcasts, heretics, impure people*—these describe what religiously correct Jews thought of the Samaritans. These people and their land were anathema, so much so that Jews would choose longer travel routes to avoid going through their territory.

Meet the third traveling man in the story: the Samaritan, the outcast. What does he do when he encounters the half-dead crime victim? He takes care of him. Actually, "takes care" is an understatement. In addition to bandaging the beating victim, the Samaritan uses his donkey to transport the man to an inn, where he proceeds to provide further care. He leaves only after instructing the innkeeper to continue caring for the man and after giving the innkeeper money to cover any expenses he might incur in providing this care.

Truly, this is a two-for-one when it comes to the moral of the story. There's the fact that the good guy is from the wrong group of people, shattering the stereotypes of Jesus's listeners. And the Samaritan's high-end care for the beat-up stranger prompts hard thinking about our own behavior and attitude. It speaks directly to the experience of so many of us who live in crowded urban habitats, with so many different types of people in so many states of conspicuous and concealed damage. The story shines light on the coping mechanisms we develop, the judgments we make, the calluses we grow, to keep those who suffer from encroaching too much on our time, our space, our agendas, our minds. Am I the Samaritan? Or the guy who strides on past the half-dead man, indifferent, self-important, and full of unwarranted confidence that I can justify my behavior, like the priest and the Levite?

If this pious pair can ignore the plight of the suffering when it's framed so starkly on this isolated stretch of Jericho Road, how much easier for us city dwellers today, in our seas of anonymous people, to disregard the stranger in need of care?

But what happens when something shifts in our sight and our hearts and the stranger becomes . . . our neighbor?

I think the philosopher Philip Kitcher gets it right when he describes the ethical challenge that has faced human beings since time immemorial. "Evolution has bequeathed to us a disposition to live together," Kitcher writes, "and a limited capacity for the necessary responsiveness to others—we can do it, but we cannot naturally do it easily or well."[4]

No, it does not come easily, and we don't do it well. This responsiveness to people—our willingness and ability to consider other people, especially those we don't know, and to comprehend the ways in which our own behavior affects them—seems sadly lacking in the human behavior I observe, including my own. The thought picture conjured by the Good Samaritan story is uncanny for speaking so poignantly to our urban lives today. It calls to mind an image from Manhattan that has been lodged in my memory for many years—an anecdote in a newspaper article about the conspicuous homelessness the borough was going through back in the 1980s. The reporter described a man lying face-down on a grate on a busy sidewalk, his ass bare, person after person stepping over him until someone, finally, had the decency to cover his butt—with a shopping bag from Saks Fifth Avenue.

This scene plays out daily for many of us, albeit in far less dramatic strokes. Certainly with the homeless people we encounter in the city, but also with our casual acquaintances and co-workers, the people who live down the hall or street. We chirp, "How are you?" We don't mean it. We don't expect real honesty—"doing well" will suffice, thank you—and we rarely have the time or interest to hear about their problems if they need to talk. Rarely do we answer honestly when the question is put to us. The incessant replay of the brush-by interaction can harden our hearts a little. But that is just one side of the coin. There's this happening, too, when we fail to see the humanness in our midst in the busy city: It makes me anonymous; it makes you anonymous. It isolates us from one another.

My straits have never been as dire as those of the man helped by the Good Samaritan. But I, too, have been on the side of the road feeling abandoned. Though not beaten to the point of being "half dead," I've been in that spot, figuratively speaking, with one problem or another afflicting me: a broken-down car, an intractable dilemma that has my thoughts in a tangle, a rejection or heartbreaking news that is making the laughing passerby and pretty blue sky seem cruel. *Will anyone notice me and my difficulty?*

Usually not—although I likely won't forget the man who stopped to help the time my wife and I had a flat tire while driving back to Portland from Seattle on Interstate 5. Standing in back of the car and struggling to figure out the tire jack—it was the first time I had encountered that particular design, and truth be told, mechanical things are not my strong suit—I fumbled and fumed while car after car after car blasted past. Just as we finally solved the puzzle of the jack and got to work on the tire, a driver did pull over and offer to help. Perhaps because of the immigration debates that had been in the news, with all the usual rhetoric about "illegals" and the wrong kinds of people infiltrating our country, I could not help but notice: From his appearance and accent, it was clear that this person was from Mexico or Central America.

Hello, Samaritan.

Do I pull over when I see a driver in distress? With rare exception, no. *It's someone else's job to do that.* So I tell myself. Isn't there a network of paid Samaritans just a cell phone call away? When we are fortunate enough to have insurance, roadside emergency coverage, mental health counselors—care providers of every sort—we do not depend as greatly on the kindness of Samaritans to help us out of trouble or distress. We call AAA when our cars die on the road; we talk to professional therapists when psychological and emotional challenges are more than we can manage.

If the solution to your problem is not covered under your

insurance policy or service plan, if the people you need are not "in network" literally or figuratively, if you don't have the money to compensate your aid giver, will you receive the help you need? Will anyone stop to help or show concern?

Too "Nice" to Care

In the Minneapolis–St. Paul area, which is where I grew up, there's a phrase to describe the way people treat one another: "Minnesota Nice." It's not always as "nice" as it sounds.

"To the locals, 'Minnesota Nice' is truly nice," observe two experts on this matter, Jerilyn Veldof and Corey Bonnema, who have written extensively on this aspect of Minnesota culture and provide resources to help newcomers navigate it. "We wave our fellow drivers through four-way stops; we help dig our neighbors out of the snow even when the wind chill is minus-forty; and we tend to be exceedingly polite. It's all good, right? Not so fast. Talk to transplants from other states and countries and you get a different story."[5]

A component of this niceness, Veldof and Bonnema explain, is a tendency to stay out of one another's business. Don't be too nosy. Give people space. Sounds fine, right? But this has a shadow side. The "Minnesota Nice" experts tell stories about people like the new guy who for two years has never been invited to a party or other social event; the person who connected with people just fine the other times he moved to a new place, but has made not a single new friend since moving to Minnesota; the workplace transferee who really needs someone to school her on office dynamics and culture, but who never receives any helpful tips—the result, no doubt, of colleagues' not wanting to have a slightly difficult conversation with her. *No, let's not intrude. We don't want to upset or embarrass anyone, do we?*

But what if someone craves and needs an "intrusion"?

This disinclination to intrude might be well intentioned (I have doubts). It also shows "a lack of interest," Veldof and Bonnema observe, "or, worse, a lack of feeling, and can lead to an even greater sense of isolation."[6]

It can. It does.

When my short-lived first marriage abruptly ended while I was in my twenties, leaving me in a state of confusion and deep disillusionment, an intrusion would have been really nice. (This divorce happened, as fate would have it, in the only year in my postcollege life when I lived in the Twin Cities.) I needed someone to talk to. For me, the compulsion to maintain a veneer of success and competence trumped all that, of course. Then, and to some degree now, a key part of my idea about myself, and what I project to friends, family, and co-workers, is my having it all together. Months passed without my mentioning the marriage disaster to certain friends. I kept the topic conspicuously absent from many conversations where it had every right to come up.

"What's new with you, Kratt?" a friend would ask.

"Not much. Getting used to my new job at the AP bureau. What about you? Have you heard the new R.E.M. album?"

Avoiding the embarrassment of my failed marriage was more important than opening myself to support. The first person with whom I seriously and honestly discussed the painful ordeal was a stranger, and she conversed with me for a fee. Nothing against psychologists and counselors; the sessions were helpful and led me to start opening up a little more with people in my life whom I wasn't paying to listen, also known as "friends and family."

Then again, some of those people in our lives probably don't want to hear about our pain and struggle. Maybe we do not want to hear about theirs. Those conversations can be awkward. Failure is not the currency that circulates in the secular city. In our workplaces and professional circles, even among our friends, it is far more pleasant and advantageous to impress everyone with chatter about how well things are going for us and how awesome our lives are.

Yes, success and status—let's stick with those! This, for many of us, is the face we want to show, the terms on which we want to be known and to know others. Yet this, too, contributes to the isolation that seems to characterize our secular urban lives. What does it have for us when our success and status take a hit, as they inevitably do?

"Insofar as modern society ever promises us access to a community, it is one centered around the worship of professional success," Alain de Botton writes. "We sense that we are brushing up against its gates when the first question we are asked at a party is 'What do you do?' . . . In these competitive pseudo-community gatherings, only a few of our attributes count as currency with which to buy the goodwill of strangers. What matters above all is what is on our business cards."[7]

What if we have nothing impressive to print on our business cards or, in fact, no business cards—a situation known as being unemployed or "between positions," as I've sometimes heard it phrased? Are we, then, *nothing*?

When the Bottom Falls Out

In this context, the ethic of Jesus is disruptive in the most welcome ways. It turns things upside down. The last are first and the first are last. What many Christians adore about Jesus is the nature of his triumph, a victory that few of us secular city sophisticates would view as much of a "win." In the New Testament telling, Jesus does not mount any thrones of political or material success—which surely he could have, given the miracle-working powers the Bible ascribes to him—but culminates his life on earth by willingly submitting to a gruesome, humiliating execution. Even his closest followers desert him in his moment of trial and pain.

How prestigious for the first Christians: *We follow the "king" who got executed on a cross!* Christians believe there's a great deal more to the story than that, of course. Resurrection, anyone? But there, too, the triumph is not one of an earthly, material nature. You will note that in the various and largely ethereal appearances Jesus makes before his disciples postresurrection, he once again racks up zero successes of a political or material nature and kicks no one's ass in revenge (despite what Mel Gibson seemed to suggest in that last moment of his movie *The Passion of the Christ*, when the risen Jesus character looks like he might go Old Testament on his persecutors).

The Jesus story is shot through with failure by earthly standards. This is good. Failures are part of life equal to, if not greater than, our impressive feats. We need to come to grips with the truth that we are flawed, that we mess up, that life will deal us blows that can be, at times, very hard to take, including that ultimate and final blow called death.

Don't play misery poker with Jesus. He'll win every time. But while it's extremely unlikely that anyone reading this book will have her hands and feet nailed to a wooden cross and be left to hang in a public place of shame while she slowly dies, we all bear crosses; we all endure pain, mistreatment, and disappointment. We tell ourselves we do not deserve these "slings and arrows of outrageous fortune," as Shakespeare called them. From advertising, from our Facebook feeds, from a million other inputs from the culture, we are told all day, every day, about all the happiness and incredible experiences and successes occurring all around us that we, too, should be enjoying.

When real life hits, the success-in-the-secular-city mode has nothing for us. This is when we can really use something to put our failure in perspective. This is when we need a philosophy and a perspective and a safety net of people who can catch us as we fall. We long for acceptance and consolation when our veneers are stripped away. We *are* going to fall. To do so with dignity and grace, and in community with people who don't judge us losers, and with a modicum of self-acceptance, is probably the biggest relief and perhaps the most impressive accomplishment of all—more impressive than our awards and raises and promotions and status-conscious clothes and résumés.

It doesn't matter whether you think Jesus is the true son of God, or whether you buy the Christian doctrine about his sacrificial death washing away your sins (and I wish to disabuse no one who believes it). The Jesus story—the humiliation, the earthly failure, the unjust execution, the dignified acceptance of all this by a figure of such wisdom and goodness—is relevant and powerful, whatever you think of its religious or supernatural components. It consoles. It teaches something important about life as it really is—not the fantasy of success and smooth sailing I want it to be.

If you're like me, the notion of Jesus as your savior, as the formula to wipe out your sin and secure your ticket to heaven, leaves you unmoved. It seems an abstraction from an interpretation of a story that no one can verify as factually accurate in all its details. Same for the idea that we can each have a personal relationship with Jesus, that Jesus will somehow be our "friend." When we are lonely, Jesus is not going to fill the empty space in the room like our best buddy, like the boyfriend or girlfriend who has broken up with us, or bring back the deceased loved one we miss so much. In the parade of indifferent strangers who pass on the busy street, Jesus is not going to suddenly pop up in the crowd, look us in the eye, and acknowledge our existence.

Or maybe he will. In a more nuanced way, I can see how the ethic of Jesus can show up, how it can address our loneliness and console us when it comes.

From being around fervent Christians so much, I have come to understand that for all their talk about the wonder-working powers of their faith, and for all their proclamations about their awesome God doing this and that in the world, they do not leave things to the supernatural. Their actions suggest they are far more grounded and realistic than their rhetoric. After an army of evangelicals have repainted a run-down public school and cleaned up the grounds, you will likely hear them exult over the wonderful thing God has just done. They can phrase it as they like. But it's *their* shirts that are drenched with sweat and *their* hands that are dirty and splattered with paint. "God" can be thought of as the driving idea, the motivating source, the ethic and the inspiration behind it all. But it was the energetic Christians who, in a sense, made the idea of God real for the benefit of the schoolkids and teachers.

In this way, I think, Jesus can be an antidote to the isolation that we perpetrate and endure in the seas of anonymous humanity in which so many of us do live. If more of us could entrench this ethic of Jesus in our brains and hearts and play it out in our daily interactions, even just a bit, the city might be a little less cold. What will this look like, exactly? I am not suggesting that those of us motivated by the concept must commit to an exact plan—fifty cents for every homeless person you see, at least five minutes of earnest listening each time you cross paths with so-and-so who lives down the hall. It's not that. It's a change-of-heart thing, a change of sight. What if we actually peered into the faces of a few of the people who pass us on the sidewalk? What if we locked eyes for a moment and gave a subtle, knowing smile? *You exist.* Even if we are not going to respond every time to the money request from the homeless guy who stands on the corner with the hard-luck story and cardboard sign, what if we looked at him, nodded, and said hi? Believe me: Seeing these faces day after day after day, truly seeing them, can begin to transform these irritating objects in our way into something quite different. Something like human beings.

Radical Hospitality

The ethic of Jesus looks like this in practice:

In Philadelphia—a place with the highest rate of deep poverty among America's ten largest cities,[8] situated in a congressional district that is ranked one of the hungriest in the United States[9]—some idealistic Christians are implementing Jesus through a project best described as "radical hospitality." The work of an organization called Broad Street Ministry, the Hospitality Collaborative feeds more than one thousand people a week, although "feeding" scarcely does justice to what happens under its auspices. The homeless and other poor and hungry people get treated like VIPs. The food is tasty and carefully prepared by an executive chef. The guests don't shuffle down a soup kitchen line but are, rather, served by a waitstaff. They are welcome to hang around for a while after they dine to check e-mail, get a change of clothes, rest somewhere more comfortable than a curb or park bench. Perhaps they are naïve, but the people who run this operation do not vet their guests for their worthiness. Are they lazy? Are they of good character? Have they done anything to *deserve* the free food and respite? Radical hospitality does not ask. Radical hospitality might be a chump, easily taken advantage of. May we all be chumps.

This is a Jesus appearance that even us nonreligious people can see and appreciate.

It is not so easy to implement. Comprehend the humanity in *everyone*? Do I really have to interrupt the misanthropic thought currents in my head and take a nanosecond to consider the possibility that the driver who just cut me off, or the pedestrian passerby with the annoyingly self-conscious hipster beard and attitude, is more than an annoying prop, more than an adversary? That he is actually a human being with worries and talents and insecurities and surprising qualities?

What if I could comprehend the humanness of the anonymous objects getting in my way on the street, in the packed aisles at Whole Foods, at the gym (oh, those inconsiderate guys who seemingly sit *for hours* between sets on the piece of equipment I want, texting their friends)? What if some of them are actually amazing? Thanks to his photo appearing in the newspaper, I learned that one of those regulars with whom I jostled for space at 24 Hour Fitness was the creative director of a major performing arts organization in our city. As it turned out, the "object" contributing to my experience of inconvenience at the gym was actually a talented person bringing artistic beauty to our city. Maybe the guy who seems to be in my way on the chest-press machine (not that I have any more right to it than he) is an incredibly warm and generous person—and would probably share the equipment with me if I asked. Maybe the woman "hogging" the mats (as the misanthrope in my head views the situation; you might call it "using") does important work to reform the education system for the benefit of poor and underserved kids. Maybe the irritant "crowding" me in the locker room—never mind that the lockers are crammed together like sardines in a can—runs a nonprofit providing humanitarian relief to war refugees.

Do you know about Jesus and the woman at the well? In pursuit of a drink of water (and something more profound, as it turns out), Jesus interacts humanely with a person whom he really ought to shun if he is going by the rules. She is officially bad in multiple ways, certainly no one with whom a proper Jewish man should speak. By the prevailing conventions, Jesus should have avoided contact because she was (a) a woman, (b) a Samaritan, and (c) an outcast in her own community, as revealed by the fact that she is drawing water not in the company of the other women, but alone and at the worst time of day. In the story, though, Jesus sees through the surface appearances, through all that marks the woman as anathema, and comprehends her humanity. He breaks taboo even further by talking with her—and, more crazy yet, by asking for a drink of water from her cup. A drink from the ritually unclean cup of a Samaritan woman? This is something a religious Jew just did not do. Jesus saw someone who was supposed to be invisible—there's your first bit of rule breaking—and then went a transgressive step further: He accepted her as a worthy human being.

Jesus even sees the humanity in the guards who are carrying out his execution and prays for their forgiveness.

It sometimes occurs to me as I go through life in the crowded secular city that I want to develop the eyes to pierce the hard surfaces and see the humanity of others, and that I want the environment in which I live to be one where people see *me* for more than my surface markers.

Even as I write that, a part of me protests. Aren't we safer behind the veneer? Who has the time, or the space in his cluttered head and hardened, nonexpandable heart, for this radical humanitarianism? But there is some other part of me, the more idealistic part—increasingly the *main* part, I'd like to think—that finds the Jesus example inspiring. I would like to behave more like that. I would like to live in a world in which that ethic prevails, in which more anonymous people in more city settings receive the treatment the Samaritan woman received from Jesus.

On reflection, I realize this has gotten inside me. As discussed earlier, in my column-writing life I have been drawn to stories that humanize the "other"—Muslims and evangelical Christians and atheists and gay people and so on. Because I am infected by the Jesus story, I find myself judging my conduct on the basis of how I treat those I could get away with *mis*treating: the VUIPS, the very *un*important people by the society's standards. I am thinking of myself as a VUIP in the large scheme of things—and finding that perfectly acceptable.

In the moments when I have expelled the misanthrope from my head—and those moments do come—I look passersby in the eyes on the crowded city sidewalk and flash a quick, knowing smile. *You exist; I exist.* Back in Portland, when I crossed paths with the immigrant woman who cleaned the public areas of our condo building, I stopped to say hi and thank her for her work. When a new person joined the staff at the college where I worked—especially if he or she was a person of color, for whom that campus, like Portland as a whole, could be a bewildering place—I made a point of learning his or her name and giving a warm greeting each time we met.

In Portland, shown by statistics to be the most secular major city in America, I developed a regard for another set of humans too few of us mountain-climbing, artisan-roast-coffee-sipping, nonreligious progressives had in our sphere of concern: the kids. Despite Portland's progressive ways, the city has high rates of child poverty and a large number of kids in the foster-care system for whom permanent homes cannot be found. Couple that with relatively low graduation rates and scant access to sports and other youth-development programs for disadvantaged kids, and you have an unjust situation—one that bodes ill for the future and that should not sit well with progressive Portland.

So when the call came to join the board of an upstart nonprofit supporting the most underprivileged elementary schools kids in Portland (at an obvious cost to my budget and "me time"), my Jesus-infected conscience told me "go." Not that I am a fan of board meetings that run past 9:00 P.M. on "school nights." But I came to be immensely proud of how this nonprofit, AC Portland, developed and contributed to kids' lives over the several years of my involvement. Hundreds of largely nonwhite kids are now playing basketball and soccer and learning about nutrition, writing, and community service in their after-school hours. They wouldn't if not for the efforts of a few determined community servants who accepted as their neighbors these kids from the proverbial wrong side of the tracks—and *treated* them like neighbors.

In this sense, maybe Jesus *is* the way, as Christians like to say. He at least *shows* the way. I am not talking about the way to an afterlife, but a way by which the annoying objects competing for space and blocking our paths become a little more human to us, and we to them. A way by which we might warm up the cold parts of life in the secular city.

Chapter Seven

INCARCERATION NATION

I wish Jesus had been there to intervene in the Kafkaesque situation that unfolded in a Michigan courtroom that day, when a struggling veteran listened to a judge scold him for not working and making money—and then proceeded to throw him in jail for his lack of money, thus costing the guy the job he had just landed. I suspect Jesus would have had something useful and challenging to say about that particular episode, as well as the many other errors of judgment and heart that have turned our criminal justice system into the unjust mess that it is.

Here's more about the ordeal of this vet, Stephen Papa, and the larger phenomena it illuminates:

The judge, after lecturing Papa and demanding that he maintain steady employment as a condition of probation, tossed the young man in jail for twenty-two days. The reason? Papa's coming up twenty-five dollars shy of the "fifty bucks" demanded as a first installment on his court bill.

Papa's mind-boggling encounter with the criminal justice system began with an admittedly stupid drunken escapade (similar, I realize, to the stupid escapades I had when I was in college and just a few years younger than Papa's twenty-seven years). The Iraq war veteran had gotten drunk with some friends and climbed to the roof of an abandoned building. Papa and pals had then slipped inside through a broken window, where they attracted the notice of police and got arrested.

Papa was struggling. He had come home to Grand Rapids, Michigan, in 2012 after serving in Iraq with the Army National Guard. Jobless and homeless, he had been sleeping on friends' couches and picking up a few dollars doing one-off jobs like building a shed for a friend's grandparents, accounting for the twenty-five dollars he had in his pocket as he went before the judge.

A sum like that won't get you very far. It got Papa nowhere with Judge Benjamin Logan, who wanted the defendant to produce $50 on the spot as a first installment on the $2,600 Papa owed for restitution, fines, and court fees. The vet tried to explain that $50 was double what he could produce at the moment—but that more money was on the way thanks to the new job he was about to start.

"Wrong answer," the judge barked. "My expectation is fifty bucks and I just sent three people to jail that didn't have it."[1]

Make it four. Well, at least Papa no longer needed to worry about finding a place to sleep for the new few weeks. Arrangements, shall we say, had been made—at the Kent County Jail.

A Prison Industrial Complex

"It baffled me." This is how Papa would later describe his reaction to the judge's behavior. *Appalled* would be an apt description of what many members of the public felt when they heard about the veteran's treatment and pondered the larger phenomenon to which it pointed. Thanks to Papa's story being told on National Public Radio, and thanks to prison reform advocates citing it as they pressed their case for change, his ordeal became something of a cause célèbre. It was emblematic of a phenomenon that had started as a seemingly sensible and necessary strategy to reduce crime but that mushroomed into a morass of unintended consequences that have made the solution as bad, or nearly so, as the problem it was engineered to solve.

We are tossing a lot of people in jail and prison in this country. Often, for a very long time. And it's taking a toll not just on the prisoners and their families and communities, but on all of us.

With the prison-reform issue gaining steam and raising public awareness in recent years, you probably have heard some of the statistics. We have a higher percentage of the population in prison than any other country on the planet—716 per 100,000, according to the 2013 numbers.[2] There is this figure, too: Although the United States has only 4.4 percent of the world's population, it has some 22 percent of the world's prisoners.[3]

The United States has become Incarceration Nation.

A crime crackdown built around longer, more rigid prison sentences has been under way for several decades now, fueled by a "tough-on-crime" phenomenon of the 1980s and '90s that swept up leading politicians on both sides of the aisle and dramatically swelled the prison population. The phenomenon has continued full steam despite declining crime rates, and despite growing awareness of the lives ruined, and vast sums of public dollars spent, in our unfettered zeal to put people away.

You might be responding at this point, *Hello, fool. Of course crime rates have gone down. This is because we've been locking up the bad guys. The tough-on-crime strategy works. It's made us all safer!*

True, to a degree. But as reform advocates point out, a large percentage of prison inmates—more than 60 percent of them in the federal penal system[4]—are in for nonviolent crimes such as drug and immigration offenses. This means that unless their experience in prison has changed them for the worse (which can happen, admittedly), they pose no real danger to our safety and property. Dealing with them through incarceration is not only counterproductive in terms of rehabilitating them but also costly—costly to the men and women who have large segments of their lives taken from them and are subjected to the brutal and dehumanizing experience of prison; costly to the families whose fathers and mothers are separated from them and prevented from contributing; and costly to a society that spends untold billions on its state and federal prison systems and that allows itself, through the course of all this, to become harder and coarser.

As the story of Stephen Papa dramatizes, some people end up in jail or prison for the offense, basically, of being poor.

A harrowing report called "The Poor Get Prison" by the

Institute for Policy Studies documents how the get-tough ethos has spawned not only stiff mandatory sentences but also the now-common practice of making defendants cough up money for bail, public defenders, probation officers, court costs, fines, electronic monitors, and other trappings of the system—to the point where these assessment strategies have become important revenue sources for some jurisdictions. In 1991 only about a quarter of inmates owed money for their processing; by 2004 the percentage had tripled. Today, an estimated 80 to 85 percent of released prisoners carry this burden with them as they undertake the difficult project of reentering society.[5]

What begins with something as trivial as driving with a broken taillight—guess which people are more likely to be doing that, the poor or the wealthy—can escalate into a nightmare of unaffordable fees, (billable) time in jail, lost jobs, families damaged, lives wrecked. If things go sideways with the officer and you happen to be black, it could even lead to your being shot. Dead.

In view of race dynamics in this country (which we will discuss more in the next chapter), you will not be surprised to learn that these phenomena fall hardest on black and brown people. Black men, in fact, have a one-in-three likelihood of being imprisoned in their lifetimes, in contrast with the one-in-seventeen figure for white men.[6] (Ever wonder why a lot of black fathers are absent from their families, as the sociologists inform us? Well, in many cases, they can't be with their children even if they want to because they're in prison.)

Behavior problems that tend to bring a medical diagnosis for white kids—ADHD and the like—are far more likely to yield a criminal "diagnosis" in schools with large percentages of black students, a 2015 study finds. As one pithy headline describes the phenomenon, "Black kids get cops, white kids get docs."[7]

Here we find the source point of the so-called schools-to-prison pipeline that has proved so efficient at turning students into inmates.

The now-popular practice of dinging you for the privilege of being processed by the criminal justice system is not a huge problem if you're a middle-class or wealthy prisoner, of course. It is a huge problem indeed if you are like many of the people in the system—poor—and have no means to pay these costs, which can escalate into many thousands of dollars.

If you don't have the dime—hundreds of thousands of them—you can pay with your time. So it goes in today's system.

In an exhaustive series on the explosion of costs being imposed on defendants, NPR found that, as of 2014, forty-three states allowed courts to charge defendants for their public defenders. Forty-one states allowed jurisdictions to charge prisoners for room and board, as if jail were some kind of hotel. In forty-four states, they could be charged for the services of their parole officers.[8] In the absence of any consistent methods and criteria for determining who is able to pay and who is not, judges often go on instinct, impressions, and whims. And often they decide to throw someone in jail, or back in jail, for the failure to pay up.

And you thought debtors' prison was a thing of the past.

Jesus in Jail?

Who said, "I was in prison, and you came to me"?

Correct. It was Jesus, in Matthew 25, to be precise. And although he meant it rhetorically, as a way of signaling his solidarity with those rotting away in jail, it wouldn't be long before he was factually a prisoner, too—a death-row prisoner at that.

This is the same Jesus who famously declares in Luke 4, as he stands in the synagogue and reads aloud the words of the Old Testament prophet Isaiah, that he was sent to proclaim release for the prisoners.

If you overlay the behavior and words of Jesus onto the reality of prisons in our time and place, you realize that although the United States is, in some ways, a Christian nation, it is not a Jesus nation when it comes to our treatment of those who have transgressed.

The Jesus way is a radically different way. The Jesus vision for crime and corrections is light-years apart from the vision we implement today. Apart, and superior. Jesus can free us from the prison-industrial complex to which we are all captive, in some shape or form, and from which we all need release.

It costs us dearly to lock up more people than any other country on the planet. There's a steep cost to our character as a society, to our collective soul as a nation. There's a distortion of our priorities and commitments. Then there's the money. Operating the federal and state prison systems costs a combined $80 billion a year, roughly.[9] The collateral costs—social services, child welfare, and so on—add billions more to the whopping total.

To put the numbers in perspective and discern the story they tell about us, consider this: Eleven states spent more of their general-funds budgets on prisons than on colleges and universities in 2013.[10] The fifty states' combined spending on their "corrections" systems grew by 141 percent between 1986 and 2013. The growth in their spending on K-through-12 and higher education: 69 percent and 6 percent, respectively.[11]

It seems we have a prison problem. As in, too much prison for too many people.

As I've written in *USA Today*, one of the most impressive forms of Christian outreach is, to my mind, prison ministry. I realize an aspect of this might make a non-Christian feel a little cynical. Who could be a more truly captive audience for evangelism than prisoners? As for me, I say that even the cynics ought to give the prison proselytizers a pass. Anyone willing to go to one of the nastiest environments imaginable and spend time with the most despised and forgotten segment of the population has probably earned the right to promote his or her religion.

The Jesus followers who visit prisoners have multiple motivations, actually. For some, it's a simple matter of compassion. For some, it's a command-and-obedience phenomenon: Their savior compels them to go; they go. At a deeper level, we can see the special resonance of prisons and prisoners with a religion whose central figure and many of its earliest practitioners and promoters found themselves in jail. Jesus was a criminal in the eyes of the authorities, a worst-of-the-worst offender who got the ultimate penalty.

This Jesus compels his followers to go to the prisoners. He identifies with them, stands in solidarity with them—without ever asking what it was that got them behind bars.

Head-turning stuff.

But what is one to *do* with it? Isn't all this freedom-for-the-prisoners stuff hopelessly unrealistic? Can't those influenced by Jesus settle for a little interpretation here—prisoner "freedom" in some symbolic sense? You know, better conditions behind bars, more people visiting inmates and showing their concern, enhanced libraries so that prisoners can free their minds, if you will. We can't actually *release* the prisoners, can we?

Of course we can. A lot of them, anyway. And we can save significant numbers of people from the downward spirals that funnel them to our prisons in the first place. By taking a cue from Jesus, by acting on the inspiration of his message in combination with good data and our ever-expanding knowledge about what works, we can challenge status quos and imagine different approaches. Who says the only way to deal with crime is to lock up the bad guys and throw away the keys?

If we created the kind of just society envisioned by Jesus, far fewer people would suffer the dysfunction and desperation and deprivation conducive to crime. A gargantuan task, for sure. But in the meantime, strategies are emerging for working with at-risk young people and returning offenders in smarter ways.

Take, for instance, the strategy for disruptive students being developed by a psychology researcher named Ross Greene. Eschewing the consequences-and-punishment strategy long used for disruptive, troubled children, opting out of reliance on suspensions, expulsions, and the like, Greene and those employing his methods are actually changing kids' behavior and lives. The strategy is especially relevant to schools and juvenile detention centers but has implications, too, for the grown-up jails to which many of those in the schools-to-prison pipeline are bound to "graduate" unless their lives are turned around.

This is not fuzzy, feel-good foolishness revolving around the wondrous magic of hugs. It's rigorous stuff based on the latest scientific understanding of the human brain. When kids act up, school personnel employing the Greene method resist the temptation to throw them out of class or administer other immediate punishments. Instead, they bookmark the incident and, after the fury of the moment, sit down with the student and unpack the situation. Why did he or she suddenly curse out the teacher? Why was it necessary, just then, for him or her to stand up and act out? The next time the impulse arises, what might be a better thing to do? What is going on in the kid's life or neurology that might be contributing to his or her behavior?

"The goal is to get to the root of the problem, not to discipline a kid for the way his brain is wired," the journalist Katherine Reynolds Lewis writes in a hopeful article on Ross Greene and his method.[12] The beauty of this approach is that it doesn't just work with and around the wiring of the brain; it can actually change that wiring.

When California woke up to the punitive foolishness of its three-strikes law, which was imprisoning people for life upon a third conviction, no matter how minor the crime, it started releasing some of these lifers. Importantly, encouragingly, the state has found the vast majority of these so-called career criminals are staying straight.[13]

These are but two examples. We could find many more, all with their promising efficacies and inevitable shortfalls. The point is that better ways exist—and more will certainly be found if the culture's abundant talent and know-how are put to the task. Ways can be devised to intervene in lives to turn current and would-be prisoners into productive citizens. Buoyed by the Jesus inspiration, following the Jesus way, we can open our minds, hearts, and eyes and look for creative ways to disrupt the prison pipeline. Our sights and imaginations can be freed from the current illusion that leads us to think that our only tool for transgressors is the hammer, and that every aspect of the phenomenon is a nail.

With Arms Unopened

Are you familiar with the character named Taystee on the Netflix series *Orange Is the New Black*? We can learn a lot from the ordeal she experiences upon her release in the series' first season. A ward of the state and foster-care system while growing up and a resident of correctional facilities from the age of sixteen, Taystee reels from disorientation and adversity when she leaves prison and tries to find her way in the world. She is utterly unequipped and underresourced. She tries to set up residence in a crowded, chaotic shared house where an acquaintance from her foster-care days is living. No one knows her, and no one seems to care about her. The strict demands of her parole leave her flummoxed.

As if to say "f—— this," she solves her problem by intentionally violating her parole and getting thrown back in the prison from whence she came. I know—it's only a TV show. But this is a fiction that tells the truth. As the fair-housing activist and writer Kimberly Grenade puts it, "Many parolees like Taystee, who have few job prospects once they are released, turn to crime in order to be sent to the one place where they are guaranteed shelter, a bed, three meals a day, and water: prison."[14]

We stack the decks against ex-offenders. Make that "returning citizens," which is the term preferred by a onetime prisoner I've gotten to know—a man who was able to access one of the few remaining prison education programs while he was incarcerated and eventually found his way to Yale Divinity School for graduate studies. The education success story of this inspiring returning citizen, George Chochos, is the exception that proves the rule, however. In the days before our current tough-on-criminals craze, prisoners could often get an education while they served their time and thus could set themselves up for decent employment after their release. Our more recent policies and growing social hardness toward prisoners have conspired to reduce prison education programs to a precious few.

When it comes to creating adversity for ex-prisoners, we apparently like to pile it on. In many states, even after you've done your time and paid your price, you can't vote, you can't get educational grants, you can't get an apartment, you can't get a driver's license, and you can't get a job. It's reminiscent of the bewildering experience of the Iraq vet described at the beginning of this chapter. You're told to stay straight and keep yourself out of jail. Then one obstacle after another is thrown in front of you to make the accomplishment of that objective all but impossible—as if the system really doesn't want you to succeed. Is it any wonder that a high percentage of returning citizens end up back in prison?

The denial of education opportunities for prisoners is not only morally questionable but fiscally imprudent. According to one study, a dollar spent on prison education programs does nearly twice as much good preventing crime as a dollar spent on more prisons, guards, and the like.[15] The lock-'em-up strategy costs more, then costs again, in a kind of unstoppable escalation. In the insightful words of the late Senator Claiborne Pell—the man after whom the federal Pell grants program for college education is named—"Diplomas are crime stoppers. It costs much less to educate a prisoner than it does to keep one behind bars."

How tragic for the men and women who end up back in prison—how foolish of us as a society—that we choose the latter.

Welcome Home

In the revered Parable of the Prodigal Son, Jesus tells the story of a young man who somehow persuades his well-to-do father to give him his inheritance in advance. The father decides it will only be fair to extend the courtesy to his other son, so he, too, is given his half of the estate. The sons pocket the same inheritance. But what they do with it is very different.

The second son—the older and more responsible one—stays on the farm and continues his hardworking ways.

The younger lad? He runs off to a distant land and blows the money on partying, on "wild living," as it's termed in the Gospel of Luke. I don't know what that would have consisted of back then, but it's easy to imagine what it might look like in our time: maybe a long-running cocaine binge, with a lot of gambling and sex and alcohol to round out the "fun."

In the Jesus story, the wayward son apparently manages to keep himself out of jail. (He might not be so lucky in our time, when drug use and possession are a common route to incarceration.) But despite escaping the clutches of the law, the partying son runs out of money, hits rock bottom, and finds himself in a situation where he must face an equally daunting judge—the father whom he has betrayed, and whose hard-earned money he has blown.

By this point, the son has apparently discovered or rediscovered a work ethic. Desperate for food, he has started feeding pigs as a farmhand for hire. His pay, and treatment, are abysmal, though. Even the pigs are eating better than he. So he decides to go home and labor on his father's farm, where he knows the servants are treated better. "If I'm going to slop pigs," he seems to say to himself, "I might as well do it back on Dad's farm, where at least I'll eat a little better." His father's wrath seems a price worth paying.

You might know what happens next. When the wayward son completes his journey home, feeling most repentant about what a scumbag he has been, he is astonished to receive not punishment, not a stern scolding and rejection, but a welcome.

His father, seeing him from a long way off as he arrives home, swells with compassion and tenderness. He runs out to meet the son, throwing his arms around him and lavishing kisses upon him. The father shouts to the servants to bring the son a fine robe to wear, a ring for his finger, new sandals for his feet. He orders them to slaughter one of the most valuable calves and prepare a celebration. "My son has been lost," he exclaims, "but now he is found!"

So extravagant! And so unfair in the eyes of the other character in this story, who has been overshadowed up to this point. The older son. The responsible son.

He's pissed. Wouldn't you be?

Contemplate how this situation looks from his vantage point. He has played by the rules, done things the right way. He's been hard at work, loyal to his dad and the farm while his brother has been off to who-knows-where, partying and blowing all that money. And what does the kid brother get for his misdeed? A reward? Gushing love and acceptance from Dad? So wrong!

"I'm the one who's been good this whole time," the responsible son must be grumbling. "How come Dad's not throwing a party for *me*? My ne'er-do-well brother—send him away, or make him live with the pigs. At least put him on some kind of probation for a while to see if he's really turned himself around. You know, let him work and sleep in the fields and then take him back after six months or something if he keeps his nose clean. The harder the probation, the better!"

The older son, as far as I can tell, is us. His attitude seems to be the same as ours when it comes to the way we regard and treat the "sons" and "daughters" in our society who have committed crimes and now seek a return to the fold.

The way the story ends, the father consoles the jealous, angry son. "Your brother was lost," the father exclaims, "and now he is found! Be happy!"

May those of us living in America today likewise be consoled, encouraged, and transformed by the return of *our* prodigal sons and daughters.

Be clear: I am not talking about men and women who return to society with more crime in mind. You will note that in the Bible story the prodigal son has not returned to his father with phony humbleness and an intention to scam him out of more money. There's been a change. He is genuinely sorry for what he has done. He has learned his lesson, and he is committed to correction.

By telling this story, and by constructing it the way he does, Jesus seems to be suggesting that when society's wayward sons and daughters return from prison with a sincere desire to get things right this time, we should not lay a ridiculous obstacle course before them. We should not treat them as outcasts and shower new adversities upon them. We should welcome them, with open arms.

Let this be the ethic that guides, at long last, a reform of our criminal justice system.

That's Us

"For decades we told ourselves that, in showing the world the most vindictive and biased version of our collective selves, we were being tough on crime. Now, it's hard to ignore the evidence that we were just being foolish and hardhearted." So writes Ellis Cose of the Pinkerton Foundation, which works to improve young people's lives in poor neighborhoods in New York City. Cose continues, "That awareness, I suspect, will not soon or easily go away. And it could lead us to conclude, as has much of the civilized world, that vindictiveness and hope rarely go together."[16]

No, they don't go together. Forced to choose, I'll go with hope over vindictiveness, hope over foolishness and hard-heartedness. Not naïve hope that would fool us into setting loose unrepentant, unreformed killers, robbers, and rapists, but wise hope that acknowledges that prisoners and prisoners-in-the-making are human beings, not throwaways, and that their lives have worth. That they have something to contribute.

Along with hope, I suggest for us on the outside a dose of humility—a medicine Jesus liked to prescribe. To paraphrase something Pope Francis said in a different context, who are we to be so judgmental? Those of us who are not in prison, how do we know we would not be committing crime and doing time if our circumstances and histories were more like those of the people in our bursting-at-the-seams prisons? Really, if you want to get technical (and many of the crimes landing people in prison nowadays are relatively "technical"), we are all criminals; we all break laws.[17] Ever sent in a tax return that was less than 100 percent accurate, even by accident? You're a criminal. Ever place a bet with a bookie? You're a criminal. Ever fudge the truth a little on a government form you filled out? You're a criminal. I could go on. "Violations are so common," the legal experts Alex Kozinski and Misha Tseytlin write, "that any attempt to go after all criminals would sweep up millions of people."[18]

Pope Francis says that when he visits prisons and juvenile detention centers, it always occurs to him that "I could be here."

So could we all.

I've been, in fact. When I was in high school, I was in the cast of a music and comedy production that performed for men in state and federal prisons. On weekends throughout the spring, and then for four or five weeks as soon as school was out in the summer, we traveled to prisons all around the Midwest to put on our show for the inmates—to show them, as the program's director liked to say, that someone actually gave a damn about them. The students in the cast met and interacted with many of the men. They helped us unload and set up the truck full of equipment that traveled with us and, in some cases, struck up mail correspondence with members of our troupe. If we didn't already have a heightened sense of empathy for prisoners, most of us developed one quickly.

That was an interaction with the prison system of which I can be proud. Not so for the two times in my fraternity days when I actually was *in* jail. During a spring-break party binge in Florida, I spent several hours in a holding cell with fifteen or twenty other sunburned idiots. I had moved my car too far into a pedestrian crosswalk at an intersection, prompting an officer to pull me over. He interrogated me, accused me of being a disrespectful Ivy League smart-ass (which I totally wasn't), asked for my car registration, and then, upon learning I did not have said registration in my possession, pointed his gun at me and arrested me.

As for the second jail experience—it happened just a few months later—I was at a music festival in Milwaukee, walking with a pack of friends in an advanced state of drunkenness, when a sharp-eyed plainclothes cop noticed me transferring a small pipe from one pocket to another. He proceeded to search me and—guess what—found marijuana. I swear, the stuff belonged to my friend! (Never mind the fact that I was the one who insisted, brilliantly, that we bring it with us into the festival.)

I was treated to a whole night in jail that time, and even received breakfast, a slab of baloney shoved between two slices of dry bread. My friends scraped together enough money to cover my costs, and I was out by late morning, the charges expunged. I shudder to think how much longer that "visit" and its trailing effects might have been were I black or Latino, had the bail and fine been more severe, had I not enjoyed the benefit of having people available to pool their money and get me out.

So I was free, and thus I have remained . . . I guess. Free is the condition, of course, large prison population notwithstanding, in which most of us find ourselves. But now that you mention it, this Jesus liberation has something for the broad sweep of us, even the majority of us who do not currently find ourselves in a cell.

Not to trivialize incarceration, but most freedom-loving Americans are "imprisoned" by something. How? We are locked up by the enormously expensive prison-industrial complex we have created, for one. We are ensnared by the cycles of violence and retribution discussed earlier in this volume, by mindless consumerism, by debts and worries, by fears and anxieties, by debilitating notions of the good life that shackle us to workaholism and to jobs that demand all our time and energy and never let us go.

Apply the concept further, and you can see how you and I are boxed in and caught up by many things—by addictions, grief, closed-mindedness, and so much more.

We are in solitary confinement, many of us, wrought by

our loneliness, our depression, our alienation from one another and our communities and our more generous selves, by social norms that command us to get what we can for ourselves and to hell with the rest.

Actual prisoners or not, we could *all* use some of that liberation Jesus has on offer.

And we can all play a part, I posit, in bringing about some of that liberation for the prisoners who languish behind bars made of real metal. It starts, I suggest, by our "giving a damn," as the director of our high school troupe used to say. It can continue as we recognize the humanity of those prisoners. We can follow the path marked by Jesus's example and go to the prisoners. We can do this by volunteering to visit or correspond with inmates; I have seen how much this can mean to them. Short of that, we can support programs that assist current and former prisoners. We can advocate for policies that take a wiser and more compassionate approach to criminal justice. Bigger picture, we can dedicate ourselves to the creation of a society (one more in sync with Jesus) free from the dysfunction and disadvantage that contribute to crime and the creation of prisoners.

As we do this, I think we'll find the prison bars start to vanish, just like the space, and the difference, between the prisoners and us fortunate people who live on the outside.

Jesus is here to free the prisoners. That's our task, too.

Chapter Eight

THE INVISIBLE AND FORGOTTEN

What the eye doesn't see the heart cannot grieve.

—An old proverb

He got the replica pistol from a friend a little while before the police arrived. In the intervening time, the twelve-year-old kid had been playing with it at the park near his home, waving it and pointing it at random people. The friend who had traded him the gun had warned him to be careful—it looks real, the friend said—but the kid had carried on as you might expect of a boy with a new toy. The bystander who called the police said the kid was "scaring the shit" out of everyone—adding that, on closer look, it appeared that the gun wielder was a youth and the weapon probably fake.

The toy indeed did look real, just as the friend said. That's the whole point of an airsoft, the type of replica gun with which Tamir Rice was playing. The friend had removed the orange safety tip, the giveaway that it was not a real gun.[1] Not that it mattered in the crucial moment. The fake gun had remained tucked in Tamir's waistband, the tip concealed, during the roughly two seconds that transpired between Officer

Timothy Loehmann jumping out of the police car just a few feet away from Tamir and his firing his very *real* gun.

For a rough sense of what was happening in Loehmann's head, and in the head of his partner, Frank Garmback, realize that they were working in a neighborhood that the Cleveland police regarded as something of a war zone. A sign in a police station in the area blared, FORWARD OPERATING BASE, a term the military uses for bases close to, or behind, enemy lines. The park they were rushing to was known as a site of frequent gang activities and fights. Not far away were memorials for two officers killed while policing in the vicinity, one in 1998 and one in 2006. So the situation was off to an ominous start before it even started—a problem that was compounded by what the dispatcher left out.

All Loehmann and Garmback were told was: Black male. Gun. No mention that the gun waver was probably a kid, and the weapon a mere toy.

Loehmann would say later that he feared for his life, that he had no choice but to shoot when Tamir failed to immediately follow orders and put up his hands. Understandable, maybe, given what appeared from the perspective of the officers to be an ultradangerous confrontation. But to the many who weren't buying Loehmann's explanation, the officers were cruel and indifferent—an impression they further conveyed by doing nothing to tend to Tamir while he lay on the ground, mortally wounded but still alive, during the four minutes that passed before the first medical people arrived. As captured on video, Tamir's fourteen-year-old sister ran to the park and tried to get to her brother—but was tackled by one of the officers and pinned to the ground, eventually handcuffed and locked in the back of the police car so that she would not disrupt procedures.

Tamir Rice died in a hospital the next morning.

You might recall the revelations and questions that emerged in the ensuing days: Why had Loehmann been so blind to the reality of the situation and so quick to shoot? Why had the department hired him in the first place when his record showed he had been dismissed from another police force for what its deputy chief had called his "dangerous lack of composure"? Why had the officers let the boy lie there, dying, without rendering assistance? Why had they manhandled Tamir's sister so roughly when she attempted to rush to her brother's side?

Hanging over everything was this question, similar to the one asked over and over in recent years in the aftermath of hundreds of other black people's "officer-involved" deaths:

Would Tamir Rice have been shot if he were white?

I offer another question for our consideration, too—one that wasn't the stuff of the mainstream media coverage and debates, but that has the potential to transform our racial conflicts. How would this situation have been different if the Jesus way were a factor in the behavior of the officers and everyone else who played a role in the buildup to, and enactment of, the deadly moment?

It would be dramatically different, I suggest. Because Jesus helps us to see race in a whole different way.

Racism's Invisible Hands

Race is a thorny issue in our society. I've had conversations with some of my fellow white people who say it shouldn't be, who say it's a hullabaloo about nothing. We elected a black man to the White House, they point out. We find African Americans in positions of prominence and power in numerous walks of life. Race is now a solved problem, they assure. Those who insist on bringing it up invariably do so to advance an agenda.

Not true.

Yes, overt, legal discrimination may be mostly a thing of the past. Yes, some African Americans are rising to the very top in politics, business, entertainment, sports, and other professions. Yes, as we know from following the news, white people in the public eye often face swift and sure ignominy if they say or do something blatantly racist.

Yet racism continues to exert a powerful force, even if its ways are less visible and overt than in decades past. Its hands may be more obscured now, but its outcomes are still conspicuous, devastating, and impossible to ignore if we care enough to look and listen.

Look at, listen to, what the economic data are telling us, for instance. Something is not right. For decades now, unemployment has been nearly twice as high among blacks as among whites. The story is much the same with respect to household income, which for whites is about double what it is for blacks. Those disparities are nothing next to this one: White household median wealth stood at nearly $142,000 in 2013; for black households, it was a paltry $11,000.[2]

And how about these other statistics? African Americans have inferior health metrics and die younger than white Americans. Blacks, on the whole, attend schools that are less well supported and, partly as a result, tend to have lower high school graduation and college attendance rates. Marriage rates, while falling for both black and white people in recent decades, are far lower among African Americans: 31 percent for blacks in the 2011 data, 56 percent for whites.[3] More than half of African American children today are living in single-parent homes—which, for obvious reasons, have much lower incomes in aggregate—whereas only 20 percent of white children are growing up in that less economically favorable situation.[4]

Add them up, and the numbers lead to an undeniable conclusion: White people and black people are, on the whole, going through dramatically different experiences of life in twenty-first-century America. Unpack the numbers, and out fall tangles of mutually reinforcing damage and disadvantage that began with slavery and have persisted through generation after generation—a phenomenon the sociologist Robert Sampson has aptly described as "compounded deprivation."[5]

The numbers are what they are. But we don't find anything close to consensus when it comes to understanding where the responsibility lies or what ought to be done. For instance, are the majority of black adults forgoing marriage (and the significant economic advantages associated with it) because of a moral failure, as some would argue, or because of economic and sociological factors that make marriage difficult and disadvantageous? Are higher percentages of blacks unemployed because they're not trying hard enough to find work, as some claim, or because they haven't had a shot at the kind of education and workplace opportunity needed for success?

I vote for the latter in both cases. Blame it on my conscious commitment to give the benefit of the doubt to those in underrepresented minority groups. Blame it on the Jesus in me. But I do not buy the argument that if some African Americans are "making it," even making it big, then it follows that *all* should be able to make it provided they work hard, take responsibility, and exercise the right values. Personal responsibility does play a part. But it does not and cannot explain away systemic racism. The decks are stacked against blacks and other people of color, making it not impossible but very difficult for many to access career success, economic and family stability, and equal status in the eyes of the law. There is a great deal to cherish in the quintessentially American ideal of pulling ourselves up by our bootstraps. But in the words of the columnist Howard Bryant, "Pulling oneself up by one's bootstraps means nothing without boots."[6]

It would take volumes to parse the mechanics and complexities. Among them: the enduring and pernicious effects of slavery and Jim Crow; the subtle biases in people's emotional and psychological responses to black and brown skin, even on the part of well-intentioned people (present company included) who would swear to the high heavens they are not racist;[7] stereotypes that link images of hoodies and young black men to violent crime; and the privilege that gives white people a leg up on society's invisible ladder.

Privilege? The notion rankles some. Maybe you. I have an acquaintance who takes great umbrage at the suggestion that he has benefited from being white. He can rightly point to the fact that his own upbringing was tough. His parents were low income and divorced. Anything he's achieved, he insists, has come against the odds, earned by the force of his will, ability, and hard work.

My childhood was no picnic, either. But I don't share this acquaintance's apparent anxiety over the likelihood that he and I benefit from white privilege. It pains me not at all to acknowledge that I gain something from being white—or enjoy the absence of *dis*advantage, if you prefer—in a society that gives you breaks, cuts you slack, and spares you extralong odds by "virtue" of light-colored skin. There is no need to be defensive or prickly about it. It doesn't mean you did not work hard for what you have. It does not make you a bad person. Better to acknowledge the privilege, then spread it, share it, and use it to benefit those without it.

Moving On?

If our eyes and minds are open, we can start to see the role that color plays in society today. But that's a big *if*. Frankly, it's easier not to see. It's easier if we can somehow forget about the struggles of those who carry the lingering burden of racism on their backs. Really, white people, don't you get sick of hearing about all this race stuff, all this trumped-up victimization? Isn't it better to point to the African American who became president, isn't it better to point to the end of legally sanctioned housing discrimination, of "whites only" swimming pools and water fountains, and declare victory?

Isn't it time we "move on"?

Premature moving on. The favorite maneuver of justice avoiders everywhere. The scourge of those left holding the bag.

The thing that justice-loving Jesus will not let us do.

I cringe when I hear the "I'm moving on" line from famous athletes and others in the public eye who have been caught cheating, or lying, or abusing other people. I propose a new rule: Henceforth, there shall be no "moving on" until we have cleaned up our messes and restored good faith with the people who have borne the injury we have caused and injustices we have wrought. Henceforth, there shall be no "moving on" until we have done our part to establish or reestablish a state of affairs where everyone can "move on" with us. Henceforth, there will be no "moving on" until we've actually taken the time to see that which our money and status and privilege allow us to leave behind, and no "moving on" until we've locked eyes with those we want to leave stranded back there.

No "moving on" until we've finally taken the time to actually *see* the inviolable worth of the human beings we make invisible and find so easy to forget.

Many of those in the large white majority in my former home city of Portland are "moving on" when it comes to race. As I learned from the African Americans I've gotten to know in Portland, this is why life can be bewildering and frustrating if you're a minority in the country's whitest major city. From this vantage point, one sees a whole lot of socially conscious people moving on—in particular, moving on to the green dream of ever-better bicycle lanes, ever-better recycling and composting, ever-better green energy and green building construction. Don't get me wrong. Environmental measures are good and vitally needed; justice is at stake with these matters, too. But they should not, and need not, come at the expense of taking care of the community's unfinished racial business, and they should not, need not, lead to racial justice being relegated again and again and again to the back burner—which is exactly what the situation looks like if you're black.

A lot of the people who *are* fighting for racial justice in my beloved former city are Christians, both black and white. And it's not like they're having to scrounge for impetus and inspiration outside their religion. This struggle is a Jesus struggle, they'll tell you; this cause is a Jesus cause. If you're following Jesus, they'll aver, you are not moving on from the race issue until you've actually seen the human beings and human lives at stake, until there's justice for those who have tasted precious little of it.

Jesus didn't cast a blind eye. Jesus didn't cover his ears to shut out the voices of those testifying to the oppression bearing down on them. It certainly would have improved his life expectancy if he had. But Jesus didn't "move on" the way he was supposed to in the eyes of the ruling authorities. He saw, he heard, he remembered the lepers and Samaritans and women and outcasts and sinners and all the others he was supposed to forget—whom even his own disciples expected him to forget—and he not only honored the humanity of the outcasts but inspired others to do so as well.

Refusing to move on when you're supposed to will make you pesky and annoying to those directing traffic. It can make you dangerous in the eyes of the authorities. The act of not budging, of refusing to shut up about injustice, can be dangerous for *you*. It certainly was for Jesus. It certainly was for those active in the civil rights movement in this country when their refusal to budge—from the whites-only lunch counter, from marching formation for the exodus across the Edmund Pettus Bridge and on to Selma—made them a threat to the white-supremacist order and subjected them to jail or beatings or worse. Some people's extreme negative reaction to today's Black Lives Matter movement reminds us that asserting African Americans' humanity is still seen as dangerous—a taste of which my colleagues and I had when our employer, Yale Divinity School, invited one of the movement's leaders to campus to speak with our students. DeRay Mckesson's visit triggered a barrage of hate mail about the speaker and the movement he helped launch—a barrage he and his compatriots face every day.

Yes, refusing to move on, refusing to stop highlighting injustice, makes you pesky, annoying, and dangerous. It's also how we create a just and fair society in which peace can eventually break out. Not the uneasy peace imposed and enforced through real or threatened violence, but the abiding peace that breaks out and *lasts* when all people's baseline rights are respected, and all people's full humanity is honored.

Sight Restored

To Darren Wilson, the humanity of Michael Brown was definitely hard to see. Remember Wilson? He was the police officer in Ferguson, Missouri, who fatally shot the eighteen-year-old Brown in the first act of a nationally televised, real-life drama that led to large protests and spawned the Black Lives Matter movement. Listen to Wilson's testimony about his encounter with Brown, and you get the sense there was a problem with his eyesight. Brown was a big man, to be sure, six-foot-four and nearly three hundred pounds. But that alone does not explain the language Wilson used to describe what he saw and experienced when he confronted Brown and attempted to arrest him—language that portrayed Brown as subhuman and *super*human at the same time, like a grizzly bear or a monster.

"When I grabbed him, the only way I can describe it is I felt like a five-year-old holding on to Hulk Hogan," the six-foot-four Wilson testified. "That's just how big he felt and how small I felt just from grasping his arm." Brown "had the most intense aggressive face," Wilson continued. "The only way I can describe it, it looked like a demon, that's how angry he looked."

Wilson literally demonized Brown.

To Wilson, Brown had the strength of a superhuman and the ferocity (and status, apparently) of an animal. What he didn't have, however, was a gun. Wilson did. Brown's corpse was left on the street in conspicuous view for four hours or so. The sight of his dead body lying there so long was deeply upsetting to the residents of the Canfield Green neighborhood where he was shot. But leaving his dead body on display was appropriate, I suppose, if the authorities were keen on framing a message, as some conjectured.

In the aftermath of the police shootings of recent years, as in other devastating moments through history, many in the African American community have looked to Jesus for consolation, and for the motivation and energy to keep on going. Why? Because there is so much to be *found* in him and his story when your status is outcast and your social standing is inferior. Because there is so much to be *drawn* from him when your experience is constantly one of being made less than fully human. Why? Because there is so much *need* for his ethic and example in a society where the majority has a hard time seeing the minority group and the individual human lives it comprises.

Jesus was apparently quite aware of our ability not to see. Explaining why he used parables to teach, he once remarked, "Though seeing, they do not see; though hearing, they do not hear or understand."

Following Jesus gives you something akin to a better prescription for your eyeglasses or contact lenses: It improves your ability to see the humanity in everyone, especially those you are trained to overlook.

Some of the most compelling commentaries I've seen on race in America today come from an African American author and activist named Lisa Sharon Harper. Riffing on race, applying the ethic of Jesus, Harper, a Christian, writes the following on the way religion has interlaced with racial injustice and the struggle to overcome it:

> The arc of the American story reveals that people of color have struggled to flourish on this soil. And at the heart of the arc is a theological lie: Black people and other people of color are simply less human than white people, and, as a result, they have less character, capacity, and calling to steward and lead. On the flip side of the same theological coin is the other lie that white people are more like God than others—uniquely equipped and called to exercise dominion on American soil.[8]

What's impressive about Jesus, Harper reveals, is that he disrupts even the religion that is supposed to be about him. Jesus does not abide any equation that would make black people only three-fifths human, as they were officially designated in the original version of the U.S. Constitution. He does not abide any dynamic that would reduce them to merely the dehumanized image of a hoodie-clad gangster with a gun.

"As followers of Jesus," Harper writes, "we are called to seek the flourishing of *all* humanity."

To do that, I contend, we must do as Jesus did—even if we are not part of the religion that worships Jesus in the manner that Harper and her fellow Christians do. We must comprehend the humanity in all and do what naturally follows: work for a society in which black and brown people are consistently treated as equal human beings. We must do this even if our skin is a paler shade and if justice comes at a cost to our power, privilege, and prerogatives.

As discussed earlier in this book, Jesus extended himself to those of the lowest social status. He was willing to incur the authorities' wrath by associating with the wrong types of people, by telling stories that promoted their equal humanity, by actually elevating them to a kind of special status whereby our regard for *them* is the ultimate measure of our character.

The Samaritans—members of whose community play starring roles in several of Jesus's most famous humanizing stories, such as the one we looked at in Chapter Six—were not just religious minorities. They were *ethnically* different. The perpetuation of their inferior status and the hatred with which they were regarded can be thought of as a kind of racism in Jesus's own community—a racism he challenged and confounded.

This is the same Jesus who famously said, referring to those who possessed the paltriest amounts of status and humanity in the eyes of the establishment and the law (which, as you know, is the aggregate experience of black people in our country today), "What you did for the least of these, you did for me."

We find this ethic shining through as well in what the Jesus implementor Paul wrote about the radical equality that must prevail in a community built around the Jesus ethic: "There is neither Jew nor Greek, there is neither slave nor free, there is no male and female, for you are all one in Christ Jesus."

Even in the midst of their enslavement, and even more powerfully so in the decades following Emancipation, African Americans were able to see in Jesus something that subverted the intentions of the masters who had used their Christianity to justify their cruel institution of slavery.[9] In a deliciously ironic twist, many slaves and former slaves found in Jesus something subversive that had not occurred to their "Christian" enslavers and oppressors. They heard in Jesus's words, as he elaborated on the Old Testament themes of exodus and liberation, as he announced he had come to "set free the oppressed," the promise that they, too, were worthy human beings, and that they, too, would be liberated.

Jesus not only models the profound act of engaging with "the other" across ethnic and religious lines (not to mention gender and class and political lines), but he shows us something about ourselves through his embarrassing, albeit ultimately redeemed, interaction with the Canaanite woman recounted in Matthew 15.

As the brief story goes, this woman is deeply distressed by the condition of her daughter. The small girl is suffering from "demon-possession," or what we may take to be some kind of severe illness. This Canaanite woman—this ethnic and religious minority, as she would be seen by Jesus's people—comes after Jesus and appeals to him, desperately, to heal her daughter.

Jesus initially responds in a quite un-Jesus-like way, ignoring her pleas. But she is not one to take no for an answer. The persistent and, evidently, nimble woman manages to scramble in front of Jesus, and now she kneels, begging, "Lord, help me."

Still, Jesus is unmoved. He dismisses her with what some parsers of this story consider an ethnic slur, saying, "It is not right to take the children's bread and throw it to the dogs."

Dog—a term of derision and dehumanization. Even Jesus, it seems, could fall prey to the ever-present human tendency to see someone only as a type—a wrong type—and not as an individual, 100 percent human person.

But then something happens in Jesus's appraisal of the situation and, evidently, in his heart. Let it be the something that happens in each of us, especially if we are white, when we are falling for the lie that we can dismiss the mistreatment of blacks as an issue for blacks to worry about, or the stigmatization of Latinos as a problem for Latinos to address, and so on. The way the story is constructed in Matthew 15, it's the woman's rejoinder in this moment that seems to bring Jesus to his humane senses. The woman, who is quick on her feet in the verbal sense as well as the ambulatory sense, points out that "even the dogs eat the crumbs that fall from the master's table." Awakened, Jesus does a quick and complete one-eighty. He praises the woman and grants her request, healing her daughter.

Not the best process, but an instructive one—with a good result in the end.

The miracle element in this story might be a deal breaker for some, of course, in this instance as in so many other Jesus stories. "Give me a break," a skeptical reader might say. "Some far-fetched miracle-healing story is supposed to transform systemic racism?" Yes, it is, I suggest. You don't have to buy into the factual accuracy of the tale to extract the larger meaning, truth, and inspiration. What does it matter whether the Canaanite woman's daughter was actually healed of her demon possession or illness—whether any of this ever occurred in any journalistic or historical sense? What's important is that the story illustrates the good things that can happen when we reject socially conditioned falsehoods about the inferiority of the ethnic and racial "others" in our world. The point is that racial healing can happen—indeed, *does* happen—when we widen our sphere of concern, of compassion, like Jesus, to encompass and embrace those we are otherwise inclined to dismiss.

This healing, we realize, can happen in ways both large-scale and small. It can happen on the micro level, within each of us and the "others" we encounter, through simple acts of friendliness and respect. It can happen on the macro level, across our whole society and world, when we allow our newly opened eyes to begin detecting what is happening politically, socially, economically, and every other way to perpetuate the disadvantage and distress of the "Canaanites" of our time and place, and when we do our part to make things better.

Like Jesus, we can be healers.

Jesus Justice

As he trod the roads of first-century Israel and Palestine, Jesus did not encounter the complex particularities that we find around race in America today. But there is no doubt whatsoever that he saw, lived, and faced these same phenomena in different forms. With insight and brave candor, he comprehended and challenged large-scale and everyday injustices.

Were he suddenly inserted into our time and place, were he to behold our structural racism and all the other forms of injustice borne by one group or another, what would Jesus have us do?

He would, I suggest, have us rehumanize these dehumanizing phenomena and the people hurt by them. He would challenge us to stand up for those oppressed people, even though we will never know the vast, vast majority of them. He would have us see them, see past the surface markers that might normally trigger our blindness, and he would enlist us, those of us who are serious about being molded and motivated by him, in the struggle to reshape our world so that these people would experience relief and release. He would compel us to see not just those people but *ourselves*, and to comprehend, frankly and honestly, what we are doing, and not doing, to contribute to the problems and solutions.

No, Jesus did not face the exact same complexities and particularities around race that we do today. But he did know about injustice and about our human tendency to avoid looking at it squarely if we're not the ones afflicted. He did know about our tendency, at our worst, to exploit injustice and benefit from it if we can.

Jesus knew, too, about the sacrifice required of those who have the most, the sacrifice he was willing to make himself—in very extreme form, actually—to stand up and speak up for those who had no voice, no agency, and no boots (or decent sandals) to pull up by the straps.

This is not the time or place for a detailed recitation of all the action that must be taken, personally, politically, and sociologically, to achieve racial justice or any of the other justices that are absent from our world today. But we can learn some things—some very important things—from the Jesus ethic and example, and let those point us in the right direction, with inspiration for the journey.

We can learn about the issues, from reliable sources. Those of us in the white majority can listen empathetically and nonjudgmentally to the stories of those in the racial minority and learn about their experiences. White people—do you know, and are you friends with, any African Americans or members of any other racial minority group? If not, don't feel bad. Your situation is quite common. Survey data show that almost 70 percent of white people interact with blacks seldom or not at all.[10] And then once you've stopped feeling bad, remedy the situation. Your life and the life of your community will benefit.

White people, we can get in the habit of extending the benefit of the doubt, along with our compassion and enlarged hearts, to those on society's fringes and lowest rungs, who are disproportionately black and brown. We can stop succumbing to the ever-present temptation to blame victims.

Sourcing Jesus, we can find the courage to sacrifice that which needs to be sacrificed if we're to be part of the solution. It might be some of our money. It might be some of our comfort. It might be some of our status. For some of us white folks, it might be our popularity—the nicey-nice relations we enjoy with other whites in our spheres, our being spared the opprobrium inevitably borne by those in the privileged set who have the temerity to upset applecarts and speak hard-to-hear truths.

Following Jesus, we can escape the denial that tells us it's okay to go on with life as usual, that suffering in one community is a problem for *that* community, no concern to us and ours. Awakened by Jesus, we can realize that we *are* our sisters' and brothers' keepers and that they are ours, that we *are* responsible to our neighbors, even those whose skin color and life experience are vastly different from our own. Galvanized by Jesus, we can act on the realization that an injustice anywhere is a threat to justice everywhere, as Martin Luther King Jr. famously said, and that the circumstances of the oppressed are *my* problem, are *your* problem, are *everyone's* problem.

Our eyes opened by the Jesus example, we can see that this is what it means to love our neighbors.

Liberation Call

The thing about newly opened eyes is that they can't quit seeing. I don't want to intimidate you—I mean, how many social problems can one person take on?—but this compassion-spreading phenomenon has applicability well beyond race. How many "others" do we fail to see?

A major concern of mine is the intergenerational justice that we find so lacking today. This is evidenced by growing loads of debt—national debt, student loan debt, credit card debt, environmental debt—that saddle younger people now and threaten to shrink their lives and possibilities in the future. The phenomenon is evoked most powerfully by climate change and our apparent inability or unwillingness as a society to face it squarely, diminishing the likelihood, more and more with each passing day, that the children and grandchildren and great-grandchildren of the current generation-in-charge will have a world and a planet that can sustain them.

There are more "others" that are likely occurring to you: the homeless, the destitute, the trafficked, and the wrongly imprisoned. Each individual, each group, suffers from some variation of the same essential human flaw: our not seeing.

Each, as Jesus shows, deserves to be seen.

I don't care what the myopia-inducing markers might be in a particular moment. The truth is the same whether we are talking about black people, brown people, Native American people, Asian people, Middle Eastern people, or people of any other ethnicity. It doesn't matter whether the people in question are male people, female people, gay people, straight people, or trans people, or whether they are Jewish people or Muslim people or Christian people, or whether they are liberal people or conservative people, or whether they are young people or old people or future-generation people. Lose the adjectives, folks. They're all *people.*

It's the ethical imperative of our time to give them the consideration, to give them the justice, that Jesus proclaimed when he was around, to which Jesus devoted himself during his too-brief career.

It's what you want and expect for you and yours. It's what I want and expect for me and mine. And none of us has it unless everyone else does, too.

No "moving on" until all of us get to go.

Chapter Nine

REAL VICTORY

As a lifelong player and fan, I understand the temptation many of us have to take our main cues in life from sports. One of the biggest lessons is captured in a famous saying associated with the five-time-champion coach Vince Lombardi: "Winning isn't everything; it's the only thing." It might surprise you, though, to learn that the UCLA football coach Henry Russell ("Red") Sanders used the sentence a good decade before Lombardi.

As the enduring resonance of Lombardi's and Sanders's words illuminate, we Americans are a people in the thrall of Almighty Victory. It's more than the fact that we prefer the thrill of winning over the agony of losing. We have made this stuff a central organizing principle of our society: the notion that the desire for victory brings out the best in us, individually and socially, and that competition for the spoils proves to be, in the final analysis, the best way to sort out good ideas and principles from bad and to elevate talent and excellence over mediocrity, whether the "field" is sports, business, or politics. We are fueled by the tantalizing prospect of the victor's rewards. We count on competition to arbitrate our affairs. Let the market decide, we say.

But is it possible we need to care less about winning, not more? Especially when the matter at hand is the exercise in shared decision making and course setting known as politics?

Of course winning is wonderful, and our zest for it is part of what has made the United States of America uniquely successful in its quarter-millennium as a nation. And *of course* there are times when all-out pursuit of partisan victory is the only option in politics. But as with all good things, when we push our lust for victory too far, when we take it out of context, when we lose sight of all other worthy principles and priorities, this good thing can become a destructive thing.

Welcome to politics as we know it today—a political culture in which we seem better at sticking it to the other side and scoring points on the political-battle scoreboard than at serving people and solving public problems, a political culture in which we are good at shouting and poor at listening. I'm sure you've noticed: Our public discourse is completely unmoored from the teaching and example of the figure at the center of our far-and-away majority religion, a man who was, in most temporal respects, a loser.

A loser in such illuminating, admirable, and applicable ways.

Willing to Lose

In his book *God's Name in Vain*, Stephen L. Carter, a law professor at Yale, tells a story about Fannie Lou Hamer, a woman who you might say was great at truth and justice but not so great at politics. This made for a revealing interaction between her and the political power brokers at the Democratic National Convention in 1964.

Hamer, an African American civil rights activist and devout Christian, appeared at the convention as the head of a contingent called the Freedom Democrats, who were challenging the all-white delegation representing Hamer's home state of Mississippi. To the party brass, Fannie Lou Hamer was a puzzle and a headache. What would it take to mollify her and those she represented? How could they "buy" her support, get her off their backs, and persuade her and her group to stop casting a pall over what was supposed to be a grand coronation for the nominee?

"The controversy terrified President Lyndon Johnson, who wanted no blot on the celebration of his nomination," Carter writes. "So he sent his vice-president-in-waiting, Hubert Humphrey, to visit Mrs. Hamer, in order to buy her off. Humphrey, believing he was undertaking a political negotiation, asked Fannie Lou Hamer what she wanted."

What would it take? The seating of two delegates from her contingent? Three?

Hamer's reply? She didn't want anything all that complicated. All she wanted, she told Humphrey, was the installation of a state of affairs in which justice prevailed for the marginalized and truth rang out across the land. Or, as Hamer laid it out for the future vice president, all she wanted was "the beginning of a new kingdom right here on earth."[1]

I suspect Humphrey wished he had been a little more specific in posing his question.[2]

A few years ago, I got to spend time with the teller of this story, Stephen L. Carter, and interview him for an article. We began the conversation at the Portland airport, where I greeted him on arrival—he was coming to town to give the law school commencement address at the campus where I then worked—and continued talking in my car as I drove him to his hotel. We began with football, of all subjects. He told me about his enjoyment of the game and his lifelong rooting for the Washington NFL team. A few days later, after he had returned to Yale, we resumed our conversation by telephone, shifting from football to Fannie—Fannie Lou Hamer.

Carter spoke convincingly about her relevance to diagnosing and curing what ails American political culture today. He wasn't advocating for a no-compromise, no-prisoners approach to politics that some might take away from the Hamer story. Rather, he was extolling the virtue of investing our hopes and fixing our sights, as Hamer did, on a prize greater than short-term victory—on the kind of prize, I might add, on which Jesus kept his sights, too. Listening to Carter, I realized that this erudite African American legal scholar and public intellectual was onto something important. Not that being competitive is bad—quite the opposite—but that our idolization of winning lies at the root of our political dysfunction.

"If we are going to have a serious democracy, we cannot think that it's only about winning," Carter told me. "I tell my students that winning is not a virtue except in war. In the rest of life, *process* is the great virtue, I believe. And so are fairness, equality, and justice, which have to do with process. When we treat politics as though all that matters is winning, we are treating it like war, which means we are treating those with whom we disagree as the enemy."[3]

As I listened, I conjured examples from recent experience. There was the Senate Republican leader who, in the aftermath of Barack Obama's election as president, declared that the opposition's strategy going forward would be making sure Obama's was a one-term presidency—not crafting and advancing a slate of bills, not tackling the public's problems, but getting a rematch with the despised Democrat president and beating him the second time around. There were all the times I had evaluated candidates on my side of the aisle not on the basis of who had the best policies and character, but who had the best shot at sticking it to those bad guys on the other side and giving me and mine a taste of sweet victory.

"Elections have taken on this exaggerated importance," Carter continued, "precisely because we have trained ourselves to believe that people on the other side are evil, that our side has to win the election because otherwise the evil people will take over. Well, I just do not believe that, and I don't think you can run a democracy that way. What you have then is not a democracy, but a deeply reactionary society that happens to hold elections."

When short-term winning is not the only thing that matters, it's amazing what becomes possible. In politics, of course, it's much of what we have lost: fair play, decency, and engaging with our political adversaries not as enemies but as fellow citizens whom we are going to have to accommodate in some fashion (not their worst ideas, but definitely *them*). What becomes possible is our ability to craft the creative solutions and political breakthroughs that happen when adversaries know they are also allies in a greater cause.

"If you look at Fannie Lou Hamer's ministry," Carter continued, "what is striking about it is her willingness to lose. It was about bringing what she saw as the voice for Christ into the debate, and if she won, she won, and if she lost, she lost. She wanted nothing for herself. She was totally prepared to go back and be the former sharecropper she had been before. That is precisely what made her ministry prophetic—the willingness to be defeated."

In the Old Testament tradition, prophets stood for big-picture justice. Apply this to practical, of-the-moment politics, and it translates into a willingness to accept less-than-thrilling setbacks and partial victories in the short term while we dedicate ourselves to the greater, long-term victory. It also makes us willing to take principled actions that might otherwise strike us as crazy.

"Consider attack ads," Carter continued. "All of us say we hate them and wish they would stop. But the only way they *will* stop is if voters decide to vote against candidates who run attack ads. . . . If we will not make that sacrifice, then I think we are silly expecting nobility from politics. We ourselves are encouraging ignobility."

Carter, in essence, is promoting the virtue of being okay with losing a near-term battle to win the long-term fight for what's right. It's the kind of victory I propose we will see as we apply to our broken politics the ethics and example of Jesus, one of history's most accomplished losers.

Love Your Enemies?

How might we achieve real victory? A good place to start is by wrestling with what it might mean to apply to our politics what is, arguably, the most perplexing and challenging thing Jesus ever taught: Love your enemies.

Here's how Jesus laid it out that day as he spoke to the people seated around him on the hilltop where he gave his Sermon on the Mount: "You have heard that it was said, 'Love your neighbor and hate your enemy.' But I tell you, love your enemies."

Who, we might ask, was the enemy to whom Jesus was referring, and who likely came to mind for his listeners? I think we can safely say the Roman occupiers and those who enabled their harsh, oppressive rule were at or near the top of the list. For Jesus's listeners, the notion of "loving" the Romans had to have been a big ask indeed. Just as it is for Democrats in our country today to imagine loving one of the Republican politicians whose words and deeds set us to fuming so regularly, and vice versa.

And who, we might wonder, was Jesus quoting in the first half of his enigmatic teaching ("You have heard that it was said . . . 'hate your enemy' ")? It is interesting to note that this *was* a school of thought with currency in Jesus's day, which scholars in our time know about thanks to the discovery of the Dead Sea Scrolls. It wasn't a teaching from the Old Testament that Jesus was overturning, or a teaching of the Pharisees or Sadducees, as we might guess. "Hate your enemies" was the credo of a sect known as the Essenes, who, while not as numerous as the Pharisees and Sadducees, were a robust and widely distributed religious community—an influential one, too, it seems, given that Jesus feels compelled to bring up and take down their teaching.

Scooting ahead to now, I don't think it will take much head-scratching before we see who is propagating the "hate your enemy" philosophy like the Essenes. It's us, and nowhere more conspicuously than in national politics. Good luck trying to get me and my liberal comrades to love whomever we are hating in a given week, whether it's the candidate who just said something awful about women or the high-profile pastor who just demeaned gay people. Not feeling any love there. Nor, I suspect, are our conservative fellow citizens feeling much love after they have witnessed the latest outrage-inducing act of what they like to call "political correctness," or inconsistent application of that favorite liberal principle of tolerance.

I am like most everyone else on this score. Yet I am also one who once found the following words tumbling out of my mouth during a lunch conversation with a prominent Portland-area Republican, with whom I was co-chairing and planning an awards dinner of the Oregon League of Minority Voters. As we mused about a misstep the state Republican party had just taken, one we agreed was likely to make it even more of a nonfactor in famously liberal Portland, I heard myself saying, "We need the Republican party to be viable and be at its best, to keep us Democrats sharp, you know? And to keep us from our worst flaws and excesses. If we're left too much to our own devices, we will probably screw things up!"

I was surprised when I heard myself say it, but I'm pretty sure it's true.

As we ponder "love your enemy," as we imagine how it would look in practice, we might begin to realize this: While it's good to find so much interest in politics in our country today, it's often the wrong kind of interest—more like the interest we take in sports, where we follow who won and who lost, who's moving up and down in the standings, where we root, root, root for our home team and *who the hell cares* what consequences are suffered by the losers. We might begin to realize that our shared public life in the ethnically and politically and every-other-way diverse United States of America is not a game of football, where I am on one particular team and I can slough off responsibility for the well-being of the team that mine is attempting to pummel at the moment.

I suggest that our concerns and responsibilities ought to extend beyond our group and our "team" when it comes to the kind of political engagement that's required if our society is going to rise to the serious challenges that face us. It doesn't have to be *our* ox that's being gored before we care.

We don't have to be part of a particular political movement or party to take its concerns seriously. We can dig beneath the rhetoric and policy ideas that make us mad and try to understand where they're coming from and what legitimate concerns and principles are driving them—and how these might somehow be accommodated.

Isn't it possible to be thankful for our political opponents? At least those who are sincere and operating in good faith? Thankful for the effect they have of putting a check on our own side's excesses and improving our vision in the areas where we have blind spots? For helping form the creative tensions that often lead to creative solutions while forestalling the possibility of our doing really stupid things? For bringing out the best in our side—if only we can stop wishing for the elimination of those pulling in the other direction?

Isn't it possible to want the best for our political adversaries, however that might be defined?

This train of thought, I suggest, begins leading to an understanding of "love your enemy" that not only promises to transform our politics for the better but is actually doable. Think about it, and you realize there is some nuance, some interpretive give, in the two key words of that Jesus imperative, *love* and *enemies*. To my conservative friends, I would point out that this doesn't mean you will vote for my side's candidates, adopt all our ideas and policy prescriptions, or show up at our events and go around hugging everyone, purring, "You were right all along. Let's have more big government!" But it does mean that you and I might strive to understand each other a bit better, and come to view each other as more than cardboard cutout figures representing everything we hate. We might even develop a measure of empathy.

As for your enemies, a funny thing happens to them when you love them, whatever that "love" might look like. What happens, you'll see, is that they shape-shift. The instant you change the way you regard them, they morph before your eyes. They are still your political opponents, but not your enemies. And that's when the larger opportunity opens to govern and make progress.

Jesus Politics

A few years ago, I received an e-mail from an old high school friend who was now a conservative Christian. She had some bones to pick with me about a column I'd written promoting the necessity of political compromise. Compromise, she scoffed—horrible idea! How can you compromise with people who are destroying the country? In a fit of idealistic madness, I challenged her to a game that I made up on the spot. I proposed that we swap acknowledgments about what was good about the other person's side and what was lame or annoying about our own. Astonishingly, she agreed to play a few rounds. She joked that it might take her a long time to dream up anything positive about liberals, but she came back, a few days later, with the interesting insight that liberals are often good at spotting large-scale problems faster than conservatives, AIDS being one prime example. "They're like canaries in the coal mine," she said. It was interesting to learn, too, that she found it annoying that the evangelical culture of which she was part tended to frown upon yoga, which she enjoyed and found beneficial. Me? I acknowledged the tendency of liberals to treat the other side with condescension, as unintelligent and ignorant, and I pointed out our failure to give due heed to values that Republicans generally favor, such as business and American exceptionalism.

Try it sometime—if you have a friend or two on the other side, that is. And if you don't, you might want to remedy that unfortunate situation. Have your own fit of idealistic madness, I suggest. Sort of like the one Jesus apparently had through the duration of his public career.

Was Jesus political? I've heard it argued every which way. Many theologically conservative Christians make the case that Jesus was, and is, a saver of people's souls, a pathway to heaven for those who assent to a set of propositions about him and his sin-cleansing powers, and that's pretty much the whole story. Not political, in other words.

On the other hand, I've heard many progressive Jesus followers and Jesus scholars argue that Jesus was inherently political, and that while he did not engage in the kinds of political activities that come to mind for us today, his message and story were at least shot through with political implications.

Like many arguments today, this one would probably go a lot better if we defined our terms, in this case *political*. There's what we might call surface politics, the stuff of which daily newspaper and cable news coverage is made: which candidate is ahead in the polls, how many votes the Senate majority leader has corralled for the budget deal, et cetera. Then there are deeper politics, having to do with, well, *deeper* things, like justice and equity and values, and with determinations of what kind of society we aspire to have.

When it came to surface politics, Jesus just didn't play. He didn't get any laws or policies changed. He didn't win for himself or his followers any kind of political authority or status. As the Bible tells it, all of this—the most lavish political riches imaginable, all the kingdoms of the world—could have been his. In Matthew and Luke, when Jesus is being tested in the wilderness, the devil offers it all. Jesus says no.

Instead, he pursued his own peculiar and humble path, one that seemed to lead to no success at all. But two thousand years later, when his paradigm-shifting philosophies form the core of the world's biggest religion, when around the world he and his teachings continue to be at the center of daily conversations and debates and scholarly inquiry and article after article and book after book, when understandings of his ethics can even be found at the heart of many political struggles and debates, can it really be said that Jesus had no influence? That his efforts were in vain?

Jesus, it seems, was holding out for a greater victory.

When it came to deeper politics, when it came to getting into the heads and hearts of his society then and our society now, Jesus won. Not in the sense that the Jesus-based "kingdom" of which Fannie Lou Hamer dreamed has ever been installed—far from it—but definitely in the sense that the ideals he espoused and modeled have never been forgotten, and that the picture he conjured of a decent and compassionate world, while never quite within reach, has never disappeared, has never stopped beckoning as the universal ideal for which Western culture strives.

So there's something important we can learn from Jesus's politics: the value of accepting short-term losses for the sake of greater victories. It's what Jim Wallis of *Sojourners* and the widely respected author James Davison Hunter (and countless others) have been arguing for years: It takes more than elections to change society, as important as elections are. It takes *movements.* It takes a willingness to accept tactical setbacks as we go about changing the underlying climate and context, the content of people's hearts and minds. And while Jesus's teachings might seem impractical and impossible to apply to our surface politics, the opposite is true if it's movements we're talking about.

It's in movements that real victory is found. Because when the context and headwinds shift, breakthroughs in surface politics become possible, too—the kinds of breakthroughs that seem so needed yet impossible in today's climate.

"Love the Sinner"

And when it comes to Jesus-style politics, I suggest it's not only the substance of what we seek to implement that matters, but how we go about doing it.

There's a line I have been hearing for years from conservative Christians: "Hate the sin, but love the sinner."

This line can usually be counted on to make liberals fume or roll their eyes.

Let me suggest, however, that conservative Christians are actually onto something with this catchphrase, and that if we can reconfigure the lingo a little, the rest of us might find it useful in transforming our interaction with our political adversaries and moving the country ahead.

Whether they use the *s*-word or not, politically aware people on all sides of the debates see plenty of "sin" when they gaze across the tracks and observe their opponents. These days, one of the most active and confused areas of mutual criticism has to do with tolerance and its opposite. Listen to liberals' complaints about conservatives and you'll notice that they're often about intolerance—intolerance of racial, religious, and sexual minorities, and intolerance of nontraditional ways of living and thinking. Listen to conservatives' complaints about liberals, and you'll find that they're often about hypocrisy on this score. To hear it from conservatives, we liberals, we who make "tolerance" such a central feature of our philosophy and brand, we who reserve such special scorn for those who violate this principle, become the worst offenders ourselves the instant anyone fails to conform to our liberal orthodoxy. How, our critics ask, can we proclaim that we are all about tolerance—and then go off and condemn anyone who disagrees with us on gay rights and other hot-button issues?

But it's not as confusing as it seems. Not if we let Jesus help us navigate this thicket.

First a word to my conservative fellow citizens who share this concern about liberal hypocrisy on the matter of tolerance:

You are right that my side can botch the implementation of the principle when we condemn—lock, stock, and barrel—the baker who won't bake for a gay wedding or the photographer who won't photograph. We mangle things when we demand the shunning of anyone who, at some point in the recent or not so recent past, has transgressed on a given issue. But overreactions of this sort do not change the larger truth. Tolerance is a worthy principle that will remain dear to progressive hearts. I hope you see that we would make a shambles of our philosophy and commitments if we tolerated *everything*. We champions of tolerance will and should tolerate most things. But do not expect us to tolerate acts of exclusion and discrimination. For those are in the category of that which we cannot and should not tolerate: that which constitutes *in*tolerance.

Sounds logical, right? But here's where it gets tough.

How then are liberals supposed to treat those whom we see as bad and benighted on issues like gay rights?

I suggest we can take a cue from Jesus and his love-your-enemy teaching. We can do this by applying the "hate the sin, love the sinner" concept in our own progressive way. What if, instead of reflexively shunning people with whom we disagree on important and divisive issues, we shunned harmful *ideas*? What if, instead of automatically hurling harsh intolerance at those with different positions and philosophies, we reserved our intolerance for individual and large-scale patterns of action and behavior? My catchphrase for this might not be as pithy as "hate the sin, love the sinner," but there's merit in it. We might say:

Don't tolerate the deed, but tolerate the person.

Or, better yet:

Hate the hate, love the hater.

I agree with the news commentator and *USA Today* columnist Kirsten Powers when she writes, "People are complicated and multifaceted. Life is not a zero-sum game. A person can have redeeming value and disagree—even vigorously and vehemently—with you on issues dear to you. We need to get back to the idea of tolerating differences and debating ideas in the public square. Perhaps it's time for both sides to give the 'bigot' bomb a rest."[4]

Perhaps so—or perhaps we should at least bring greater care and precision to our use of the incendiary term. And perhaps we should do as Jesus taught and realize that even those political "enemies" who piss us off on a daily basis might be products of their environments, misinformation, and a whole host of other factors, and not purely wicked people with black hearts—and that every now and then they might be at least partially right.

I recommend we follow the path Jesus blazed when he consorted hospitably with tax collectors, as he is said to have done. In Roman times, these tax collectors were despised for the money they siphoned and the larger pattern of oppression they represented, all of which Jesus heartily condemned. Jesus did not abide the abuse and exploitation. He hated the hate, you might say. But never the hater.

Redefining Our Enemies

So if you're buying what I'm selling up to this point, you might be engaging in anticipatory mourning over the loss of some people who have played an important role in your world. You might be sensing the possibility of a hole in your life where there used to be those enemies you loved to hate.

I don't know—maybe there's some immutable formula in the universe that dictates that we always need enemies. Don't worry. I have new enemies to suggest! But you're going to have to accept a change in the nature of these enemies. They are not "whos," you see but, rather, "whats."

I've said to myself innumerable times, *Okay, so maybe the human race has always needed enemies and always will. But what if we could somehow transcend the idea that our enemies are always* people*? What if we could shift the paradigm and realize that our real enemies are the common threats to our having a decent world—or having a world at all?*

The widely respected social psychologist Jonathan Haidt

gave a fascinating TED talk espousing the same basic principle: "How Common Threats Can Make Common (Political) Ground." I urge you to watch it on your computer or phone.[5] When you do, you'll see that Haidt names four threats to our world: climate change, government debt, a growing inequality that erodes social solidarity, and the breakdown of the institution of marriage.

Haidt sets up his talk by imagining a scenario in which a pack of asteroids are hurtling closer and closer to Earth and are projected to smash into the United States within fifty years; the asteroids, he later reveals, represent his four common threats. When I've run these kinds of thought experiments through my head over the years, I've imagined that an alien invasion would be the kind of thing that could unite the human race. You might plug something else into the threat-against-humanity equation if you wish. Haidt's asteroids work well. So do scenarios like the spread of a deadly supergerm, or a killer hack with the power to bring down all the computers and electrical grids, or a change in the chemical composition of the atmosphere. (Whoops, that last one is neither fictional nor metaphorical.)

The point is, if indeed it's true that human nature is such that we are always and inherently in need of enemies, let's choose them well. Let's choose asteroids or Martians or killer germs and the real-life things they might represent. There are plenty to pick from! We can start with Haidt's four-item list. I'll endorse his suggestions, even though, as he points out, two of them (debt and the decline of marriage) are threats that liberals are generally loath to lament. To them I will add threat-to-humanity patterns and phenomena like tribalism, hatred, war, violent ideologies, intolerance of "the other," head-in-the-sand denialism, and our age-old tendency to choose the wrong enemies, namely those of the human variety.

This changes how we engage in the political tussles that are a fact of life. It changes them in a way that makes them fit, more closely, the Jesus vision for the way things ought to go in this tumultuous venue called "politics." *Of course* we must still fight—tooth and nail and all that!—for our political principles and priorities. But going back to Stephen L. Carter, we will be better served to remember that process matters as much as outcomes. Our tactics and our treatment of our foes must accord with the principles and ethos we are trying to implement. So in pursuit of a more compassionate and fair and tolerant society, those on my liberal side of the tracks must model compassion and fairness and tolerance in the way we engage our opponents. My conservative brethren—admirable in their promotion of virtue in society—are similarly obliged to model virtue in their political pursuits and in their dealings with their political opponents.

Yes, tooth and nail. But let's reserve most of the teeth and all of the nails, especially the heavy-artillery ones, for the real enemies. And because they are not human, we can suspend the Jesus teaching about loving them. We can hate them, in fact, and go after them with all our venom.

Who cares if I beat my human political opponent in the tactical moment at hand when pulling back the camera a bit reveals that we're both on a boat—I think it's called the *Titanic*—and it's going down?

If we are going to look to sports as our guide, let's pull out the more instructive truth they tell. Even the owners of the National Football League seem to know that Vince Lombardi and Red Sanders were wrong in enshrining winning as the Only Thing That Matters—or they are aware, at least, that this applies only to the game happening on the field on a given Sunday. When we look at what is really going on with pro football, we might realize that even though the players on the opposing teams literally knock the sense out of one another for three hours on Sunday (and Thursday, and Monday), they are all in it together in the final analysis. That's because no individual team has any standing or any meaning or any possibility of winning any championship if it's not part of an organization of other teams, what we call a "league." And no league is worth paying attention to if only one or two of the franchises have the resources to form viable teams. Imagine if this coming Sunday the New England Patriots were scheduled to play a ragtag crew that a few guys had slapped together just last week—no proper plays or uniforms or anything. Would you pay money to watch *that*?

Behold the irony at the heart of what is supposedly the most purely competitive sector of our society, an irony that is especially poignant in Lombardi's sport, which of all our major sports leagues is said to have the strictest and most "socialistic" revenue sharing, salary caps, and other structures to ensure a level playing field for all thirty-two teams. Despite what may appear to be the case on Sunday, the teams truly are in common cause. I guarantee you they would fight as one team, together, if suddenly Congress were considering draconian legislation regulating their league, or if a different sport started to seriously cut into football's dominance. As it turns out, what each team is trying to do on the ultimate bottom line is not to win the Super Bowl for itself but to advance the shared cause, one at which they have been, together, wildly successful: achieving and maintaining the colossal success of professional football.[6]

Let it be so with the Republicans and Democrats, with the conservatives and liberals, who are out there fighting on this very day for their candidates and agendas but who truly share, like the Packers and the Colts and the Patriots and insert your favorite team here, a higher objective that we see when we pull back the camera—especially if we look through the lens of one of history's wisest and most passionate lovers of humanity, Jesus.

It's all about the people—the "team" that my theologian friend Paul Louis Metzger calls "global humanity," the one human race. Improving our common lot, staving off the real threats to our species, our dignity, our humanity—that's what we are ultimately fighting for.

You can have that little thrill you get from seeing your preferred candidate shoot up in the polls or your favorite ignorant meanie get taken down by Rachel Maddow. Me? I like those things, too. But I'm holding out now. I'm okay with losing the battle if I can be part of winning the greater war. I'd rather have the long-view triumph, the big-picture win, the Jesus-style success.

I'm holding out for some *real* victory.

Chapter Ten

FOUND IN TRANSLATION

In the formulations of modern-era apologetics, the evidence from the Bible leaves the prospective believer with but three possible conclusions about who Jesus was. When they make their "case for Christ," as it's sometimes known, evangelists tell us we must pick one of the following conclusions about Jesus after considering the claims he is reported to have made in the gospels. We must decide whether he was

A. lunatic
B. liar
C. Lord

Which do I choose? you ask.

I'll go with D.

I know, I know. That's not one of the choices. But there should be a D, it seems to me, and an E and an F, too. And maybe more.

The "lunatic, liar, or Lord" formulation is something I've been hearing since my one-year dalliance with Campus

Crusade for Christ as an undergraduate. Of course, this construction, this "trilemma," predates the 1980s-era Campus Crusade. The revered Christian writer C. S. Lewis used it in the mid-1900s, and references to it can be found going all the way back to the nineteenth century. As one preacher put it back then, "Christ either deceived mankind by conscious fraud, or He was Himself deluded and self-deceived, or He was Divine. There is no getting out of this trilemma. It is inexorable."[1]

Of course there is a way out. And *of course* this preacher and other users of the trilemma method frame the matter this way for a rhetorical reason. They are trying to convince us of something, and it's often a technique of persuaders to group the desired conclusion with unattractive alternatives. Before our current, increasingly post-Christian time, who would want to incur the scorn of society by having the temerity to suggest that Jesus was lying or crazy? But this formulation, however effective it might have been in the past in convincing people to become Christians, leaves the skeptic, the doubting Thomas, wanting more options.

In view of what we have explored in the foregoing pages, let's consider some.

Popular, nonacademic writings about matters such as these often strive to be catchy and easily remembered. Let's go with that flow and try to continue the alliteration. So *L* is the letter? If we are not willing to limit Jesus's identity to lunatic, liar, or Lord, we might try the following *L* word, one I've seen used by writers including Bart Ehrman, the author of several popular books challenging the inerrancy of the Bible and the reliability of its portrayal of Jesus as divine. That word is *legend*.

The proposition that Jesus and his greatness are a legend is sure to annoy, if not anger, those with a more passionate relationship with Christian orthodoxy. *Legend*—the word refers to something that is not factually true, doesn't it? By dictionary definition, a legend is a story that is nonhistorical; that is to say, it is unverifiable, handed down by tradition. If Ehrman were here at the moment, he would probably explain that a lot of time passed between Jesus's lifetime and the composition of the official, written accounts of his life, meaning that for decades the oral tradition was all there was.

The "legend" conclusion is not as insulting as it might appear to some. Bear in mind that there is nothing wrong with legends. Indeed, to say something or someone is a legend is a compliment. Human societies have long looked to legends as bearers of moral and philosophical truths, as ways to convey important understandings of what it means to be exemplary people and live good lives.

Legend—not bad. But for the purposes of this book, where we are focusing on what Jesus can be to us today, whether we are Christian or not, other possibilities beckon.

In the midst of some lunchtime banter about *L* words for Jesus, my friend Chris asked for permission to be more creative about the *order* of letters, and to offer a word that *ends* in *l*. Chris, who is an atheist, by the way, said his word for Jesus would be *model*—the idea being that Jesus is a model for a meaningful and ethical life. I walked away from our lunch thinking about other words for Jesus ending in *l*, and one came to me: *ideal*. As in, Jesus shows us an ideal set of ethics and an ideal way to live.

Continuing with these *L* words for Jesus—preferably one

that actually *begins* with *L*—I realize there is another obvious word, one that might be the best of all: *leader.* As in, Jesus, as an embodiment of unusually wise and transformational teachings, can be a leader for us today, whatever our convictions about his cosmological nature and standing.

Lord, legend, model, ideal, leader . . . a case can be made for all of these, I suppose, and I hope the conversations continue. But what interests me most at the moment is what I am to do about it. And this much is clear: There is something in this figure of Jesus that is challenging, compelling, and worth taking to heart.

Translation Road

I'll leave it to the Christian apologists to carry on with the alliterative arguments for Jesus as lord and savior. To the scholars and theologians I'll entrust the task of continuing to explore who or what Jesus was in the theological sense—divine? human? a combination?—and the never-settled debates about things like trinitarianism, premillennial dispensationalism, substitutionary atonement, soteriology, and all the rest. And, please, argue all you want about the existence and nature of heaven and hell, and in what sense we go to one or the other, depending on whether we accept Jesus, and what this acceptance actually consists of.

Me? I am keen for the time being to take a break from learning and debating *about* Jesus and *who he was,* cosmologically speaking, and am more interested in focusing on *what he said and did* and what we can *learn from it,* whatever our location on the theological spectrum. The previous chapters have conveyed, I hope, some sense of what that might look like.

But there is a question we must address now, an ostensible problem for those like me, and possibly you, who are not part of, and not likely to be joining, the religion Jesus practiced (Judaism) or the one built around him (Christianity), but who feel compelled to follow this leader. It's the conundrum at the heart of this book.

Jesus's story was remembered, consolidated, and carried forward by religion. Many of his teachings are about God and religious concepts like eternal life. His most celebrated actions are supernatural deeds that we are supposed to regard as evidence of his status as the divine son of God—including, of course, the rather impressive feat of his dying in such a way as to cleanse the sins of humankind and then, as the Bible tells it, literally rising from the dead.

In view of all this, how can one claim to be a *secular* follower of Jesus? You can't just pluck Jesus out of religion and engage him as a sage and inspirational leader, can you? You can't just choose the parts of Jesus that resonate with the secular mind and philosophy and skip over the religious stuff, can you? If you don't accept the authority of the religious claims by him and about him, you cannot accept his ethic and example as authoritative either, can you?

The answer to all these is that *of course* you can. And, as it turns out, you don't need to.

Of course you can do all this because, frankly, there is no one or no thing to stop you. If you go down this thought path for very long, you realize that the penalty for incorrect belief, for heresy, is only a factor in religious communities or on their periphery. If you are not part of a church, and don't seek the approval or acceptance of one, how can you be rejected for incorrect belief? Who or what can tell you what is allowed and what is not when it comes to your engagement with Jesus? These realities bespeak a radical freedom for nonreligious people to engage with Jesus as we wish, with nothing like the acceptance or rejection of human religious institutions at stake. As for the *divine* acceptance or rejection that concerns religious people, that, too, is a nonissue when one does not perceive the existence of the God that administers these divine judgments. This radical freedom can be deeply problematic, as we will explore in the epilogue, which follows. But for the part of the conversation we are having now, there is only good news. When it comes to a secular engagement with Jesus, we can pick and choose, accept and reject, mix and match, however we wish.

There is good news, too, however, for those who appreciate the value of context and who, for the sake of the most robust rendering of the story, would prefer not to cut out all the religious stuff, like a postmodern-day Thomas Jefferson, scissors in hand, literally snipping away the supernatural parts. (The doubters always seem to be called Thomas, don't they?) We can keep the context. We can do this by undertaking the work I realize I have been doing since the fateful conversation I had with my father as a seventeen-year-old, when I declared, clumsily, that the supernatural claims by and about Jesus *might as well be true* because they conveyed "truths" of a different kind.

We can, simply, do a bit of translating.

Put your mind to the task, and you begin to find that the Christian context of the Jesus story need not be all that off-putting. There are ways of thinking of all the major concepts—God, salvation, sin, resurrection, and so on—that make them plausible and instructive even to the secular mind.

You want to try?

Okay. How about the religious claim that Jesus is the son of God? How can we translate that? No problem. First clue: The Roman Empire that Jesus confronted also declared some to be sons of God—their emperors. We can think of this as a signifier, a way to mark someone as unusually good and important—good and important to the maximum degree—and someone to whom special attention should be paid and special authority granted. We can see "son of God" as a signifier not just of a person's greatness but of the greatness of the worldview and set of principles he or she embodies and advances. We can see that bestowing the "son of God" title upon Jesus, over and against the temporal empire and emperors, is a way of saying, "No, it's not *those* values that are going to triumph and prevail. It's *these* values that will have the final word!"

More, we can see, as Hubert Dreyfus and Sean Dorrance Kelly do in their secular philosophy book *All Things Shining*, that Jesus had "super" powers. As Dreyfus and Kelly put it, "As he is described in the gospel, Jesus totally transforms people's understanding of what it means to be a human being. This is a super human thing to do."[2]

You can see how this translating works.

What, then, are we to make of the "God" part of the Jesus story and Jesus teachings? Isn't that a deal breaker for seculars?

Here, too, we can find a way of processing the word or idea to make it work for the secular mind. One way is by translating "God" to mean the mysterious great something that is beyond our understanding even in our ultrascientific age. (And if you think science has figured out everything, check out what's happening in quantum physics, where each new discovery seems to challenge previous understandings and remind us of how much more there is to learn.) In addition to that, we can take *God* to be a word for ultimate goodness, ultimate reality, ultimate wisdom—not bound up in concepts of an objectively real supernatural supreme being that we anthropomorphize, but something that exists in the way that ideas exist, in the way that love exists. We can take *God* to mean that which is the ideal, and we can take Jesus to be the "son" or quintessential embodiment of—the way toward—that ultimate wisdom.

Jesus "saves" us? Sure, in the ways we discussed back in Chapter Five. He saves us, if we follow his ways, from a life of futile self-seeking and trivial pursuits.

What of "sin"? There is no concept that is more hardcore Christian than that, right? Surely, a secular mind cannot wrap itself around sin.

Yes, it can. I suspect most secular people believe in sin, too—in the following way: Bad things happen in the world. People do a lot of horrible stuff (as do large-scale systems and structures). Not to say people are all bad and only bad—you might agree with me that they can be, and often are, good, too—but over the long sweep of human history we can see an enduring capacity in people to do cruel, horrible things, in ways that cause suffering and misery, sometimes on a massive scale. We don't need to believe in the literal truth of the story of Adam and Eve and the snake and the apple and the unleashing of original sin to see the accuracy of the term *sin* in describing something important and persistent about human nature. Evil—the capacity for it and the persistent enactment of it by human hands—is an undeniable reality. I don't mind if some call it "sin." And I don't mind if someone claims Jesus died for these sins because, truly, this human capacity for cruelty is what killed him, and this human capacity for cruelty is what he sought to transform.

Over the years, I have walked quite a way down Translation Road. I have found secular ways of understanding most of the major Christian concepts. I have even come to see ways in which Christian-style praying can be said to "work," although definitely not in the sense that petitioners, even those with the most advanced praying techniques, can persuade the awesome, white-bearded string puller in the sky to give them the desires of their hearts. I *have* come to see, however, that the wisest and most sincere petitioners do receive the desires of their hearts—because praying *changes* those desires.

Resurrection for Seculars

We could go on all day with our translation of Christian and religious concepts. Heaven, hell, the Holy Spirit, the forgiveness of sins—there is much more to discuss! But for now, I suggest we conclude this exercise by focusing on what may be the most important religious claim of all when it comes to Jesus—and, for seculars, possibly the most problematic: the assertion that he rose from the dead and that it's from this that he derives his authority.

It's a fascinating conversation. The most surprising and

useful secular commentary I have encountered on the resurrection and its attendant Easter story comes courtesy of the insightful Alain de Botton. Writing on the Philosophers' Mail website, de Botton takes up the issue of resurrection in a manner that deserves to be quoted at length:

> Easter commemorates an incident of catastrophic failure. The story is dismal in the extreme: [Jesus] was gentle, generous, sincere, and wise. He was close to his mother and a friend to the poor and the lonely. He believed in love and forgiveness. He understood suffering and wanted to make a better world. And yet it all ended in humiliation, betrayal, and unbearable pain. One of his best friends denounced him. He was tried on trumped up charges. His community abandoned him. The crowds jeered.
>
> Life couldn't go any more wrong than this.
>
> Jesus of Nazareth was nailed up on a cross and left to die. He suffered the fate of a criminal and an outcast. (For a long time,) no one really gave a damn.
>
> Who knows if it really all happened like this? But that's not really the point. The truth of the story isn't the decisive factor. He was clearly not "the son of God," but the story nevertheless retains a critical power to educate the modern world about one or two important things.
>
> Jesus is a symbolic character, a representative human being. No one is like him all the time. But most of us are a little bit like him some of the time. The story of his suffering is a strategically exaggerated version of the griefs involved in human experience

more generally. Terrible things happen. Cancer is diagnosed. A divorce shatters a family. A firm goes bankrupt. An ordinary mistake triggers a calamity. A parent dies before a child gets around to sorting out what they might have meant to them.

Holding up the story of the Crucifixion for regular contemplation makes the most painful scenarios feel more familiar and more normal; severe trials and periods of misery are written into the contract of life.

Yet in a lot of today's individualistic narratives, defeat can only be explained by a person's own weakness or stupidity. Those who fail are callously described as "losers." We are taken to deserve our fates. Against such a punitive backdrop, the story of the Crucifixion emerges as offering a more endurable and forgiving map of life.

It was the genius of Christianity to insist on making its central figure an "ordinary" person, not an idealized all-powerful deity, but a character exposed to every available indignity—and at the same time, to insist on his status: both the king of kings and an ordinary loser. This was a truly revolutionary move with a deeply consoling message at its heart.

What is the mark of a good life? Who should be considered a success? Easter offers a surprising and helpful answer: success is not about obvious worldly triumph, it's about developing an ability to use one's own suffering as a route to compassion for others.[3]

Jesus's story indeed was a tale of woe, but one with a stirring triumph at the end—a triumph that even secular minds can appreciate. For as de Botton notes, the symbolic truth is deep, compelling, consoling, and as close to universal as anything you might find on the postmodern landscape. Let compassion reign!

De Botton is also correct when he notes in the same article that the most "boring" question we can ask about religion is whether it is true. To the secular mind, it cannot be true the way we expect a textbook to be accurate or "true." But as de Botton goes on to write, this might not be a reason "to dismiss the religion in its entirety, just as one wouldn't disregard *Anna Karenina* on the grounds that the tale had been somewhat invented. Religions are intermittently too interesting, wise, and consoling to be abandoned to believers' alone."

That is why it is entirely valid and incredibly helpful for seculars to engage with this story. Not because we believe Jesus to be literally divine, someone who is worth listening to and emulating because he is God. Rather, we can do so because our senses and wisdom and lived experience and openness to inspiration help us see that there is something valuable in all this—help us see that Jesus and this story are *extraordinary*, both literally and in the colloquial sense of that word.

Does Jesus have a claim on us? Maybe so. Not because he's the cosmologically anointed savior. But because he's right about the world in really important ways, and it's of great benefit to us, and our world, to heed his teachings. And even though we seculars will never be caught dead talking about things like the "body and blood" of Christ and symbolically partaking of them, I hope you can see that it's not a bad idea, not a bad idea at all, to think about how we might in some sense internalize what he stood for.

Yes, there are robust ways in which we can find elevation in the story of the resurrection. In the words of my religion-writing coconspirator Brandon Ambrosino, "What's radical about Easter . . . is not that Christians claim a dead man rose from the dead. What's radical is what that means—specifically, what it meant for Rome, and, by implication, what it means for all kingdoms everywhere, including the ones we live in."[4]

A resurrection conversation is well worth having. Not like the argument that's been carried on since time immemorial about whether Jesus literally rose from the dead and what kind of form he assumed postresurrection, but a conversation about the symbolic and ethical meaning of that resurrection—of that transformation—and what it might offer to us today, individually and collectively.

How are we going to live our lives? To what ultimate ends are we devoting ourselves? What bottom-line ethic is going to inform the countless decisions we make and actions we take, as individuals and together?

These are the kinds of questions worth asking if our lives are going to be fully lived. And while the Jesus story is far from the only place where we can find insights and inspiration, it's an extraordinarily good place to go looking.

It's interesting and encouraging to see ways in which Jesus insights can pop up, even in secular circles. Case in point: the way the words and deeds of Pope Francis got New York Mayor Bill de Blasio, a generally secular liberal, to see the Sermon on the Mount and its deliverer with new eyes.

As the mayor told *The New York Times*, "The Sermon on the Mount, to me, is as good a summation of my values as I could possibly imagine." But since the time of its telling, de Blasio went on to say, "a lot of things happened that caused so many of us to doubt, or be confused."[5]

Yes, a lot of things did happen to sow doubt and confusion. Among them: disputes over doctrine and politics, profound changes in the context, and the development of a lot of cultural baggage and off-putting representations of Jesus that caused him—for de Blasio, for me, and maybe for you—to be lost in translation.

But what was lost in one translation can be found in another.

It's good that de Blasio is apparently navigating the doubt and confusion now and finding his way to something valuable in the Sermon on the Mount and the figure to whom it is attributed. I hope many others are, too, because these values espoused by Jesus in that sermon for the ages, as in so many other instances and ways, are what the world needs now.

Yes, I am a Doubting Thomas who has gone a long way down Translation Road, and although there is still plenty of confusion in my head, and all sorts of doubt, there is enough that's clear. Down that road I think I've found an answer to the question Jesus asks in Matthew 16:15: "Who do you say that I am?" What I've found is not exactly the savior of Christian understanding. What I've found is not in the lunatic-liar-Lord lineup from which C. S. Lewis and the other apologists want me to choose. But what I've found is quite valuable and transformative.

Jesus is someone worth following.

Epilogue

JESUS AND HUMANS AT YALE

When the "WTF?" discussion group convenes on the fourth Monday of every month, in a meeting place three blocks from the campus of vaunted Yale University, we talk about heavy stuff. Dissatisfied with the premise that we nonreligious people pretty much wing it when it comes to the purpose of life and doing the right things, rejecting the notion that seculars like us must always go it alone and start from scratch in constructing good and coherent lives, we (along with the two or three Christians who often join us) come together to address the question captured in that classy three-letter acronym we use as the name for our group:

Who, or what, to follow?

It's a good question. Twitter uses the phrase, too, which I realized a week or so after I thought of it as the name for our discussion group. In fact, it's posed quite prominently on Twitter, in the upper corner, beneath which you find a listing of three Twitter accounts you might want to add to your "follow" list. There's apparently a clever algorithm that figures out which tweeters to suggest to you in that prime section of the page. I have found that some of these people actually are worth following—in the Twitter sense. But at WTF? we are interested in "whos" and "whats" with more heft and follow-worthiness than most of the people on Twitter (notwithstanding the various Jesuses you'll find there, including @Jesus and @Jesus_M_Christ). And we explore a form of "following" that goes a lot further and deeper than allowing someone's tweets to appear on your feed.

The regulars and semiregulars at WTF? are an eclectic and conscientious bunch. At the time of my writing this, there was Chris, the executive director of the Yale Humanist Community (which hosts the discussions) and the author of a well-known book that lays the groundwork for a form of secular life that is friendly to religious people and open to collaborating with religious organizations.[1] There was Wendy, who expresses her humanist values through her headlong commitment to serving the community and the world. There was Jonathan, a twenty-something activist and advocate for paraplegics and quadriplegics. There was Lamont, the one-time front man of a well-known Christian rock band who is somewhere in the post-Christian-but-still-inspired-by-Jesus neighborhood, now devoting his career to filmmaking in support of humanitarian causes while still playing music. There was Stephen, the Yale Humanist Community intern and an atheist who is studying for his master of divinity degree at Yale. There was Erika, an author and "life artist," as she accurately describes herself. There was Matt, the pastor of an area evangelical church who is also a Yale instructor and a prize-winning theologian with three Yale degrees. Some weeks, there were others. And there was me, the one whom Chris invited to start and lead the discussion group after I told him I was developing the crazy idea of being a secular Jesus follower. Me, the guy who came up with that catchy name for our group, which I hope you like.

I wonder what William F. Buckley would think.

Buckley, as you may know, wrote a seminal book back in 1951 called *God and Man at Yale,* which in many ways presaged what has become a standard conservative critique of the liberal, secular university and the larger liberal, secular world that places like Yale epitomize. When the book came out, Buckley was a freshly minted Yale graduate bound for prominence as a leader of the conservative movement. To great pushback and criticism, the book argued that Yale had become antireligion, anti–individual rights, and antithetical to the convictions and aspirations of its more tradition-revering alumni.

I suspect that those who share the Buckley worldview and who are alarmed by today's advancing secularity would not be greatly reassured by what's happening in our small circle on the outskirts of Buckley's alma mater. At the Yale Humanist Community, as at our WTF? discussion group, most of us are decidedly nonreligious and experiencing no angst over our lack of conventional belief. Although we want to become more intentional about our values and ethics, we perceive and lament no God-size holes in our lives. We appreciate our Christian regulars and semiregulars being candid about their beliefs—after all, friendly and open engagement with religious people is part of our credo—but at WTF? our religious friends engage on a secular level, too, never vocally assuming or asserting the superiority of their theistic belief system.

If we are not talking about God at our WTF? discussion

group, what are we talking about? Just little things like life, meaning, ethics, and changes we have made or have failed to make in our lives based on the figures and philosophies we find most worthy of following. We talk about what it means to follow someone or something, both conceptually and in practice. We acknowledge that the very act of following cuts against the grain of a secular ethos that encourages fierce independence of thought, and of a society that exalts leaders, not followers. We know that the idea of following conflicts with the intellectual and academic trains of thought on which most of us generally ride, where we are more inclined to study and analyze figures and philosophies than to apply them, where we are more comfortable learning *about* things or people than learning *from* them. What does it mean, we ask, to place our trust in a figure or philosophy and to *go with it* even if we haven't necessarily measured and mastered all the angles? What do we gain and what do we risk when we suspend our detachment and critical thinking and internalize something in a way that might change us? Who or what are we following? What does it mean, in practice, to follow the particular people or schools of thought we have chosen?

So those are the little things we discuss at our WTF? discussion group—and, often, Jesus. So much so, in fact, that I keep threatening to create bracelets for us all modeled on those WWJD—"What Would Jesus Do?"—bracelets that were popular in the 1990s. The lettering on ours would have a twist, of course. I think you can sense where I am going with this. Say it with me now: W-T-F-W-J-D.

Not only do group members tolerate my bringing up Jesus in these discussions, but many of them like to talk about him, too—and not just the handful of Christians. We talk about what it would look like to actually implement the more inspiring and intimidating Jesus exhortations. Among those that come up are his teaching to eschew a fixation on material acquisition (and the tendency to stress out over money, time, and other scarce resources), his call to love our enemies, and his insistence that we extend radical generosity and hospitality, even to the people who make us want to run in the opposite direction.

We juxtapose Jesus with our tendency, if we don't watch ourselves, to engage with people—even those closest to us—on a transactional, instrumental level rather than as real, live human beings whom we are compelled to . . . um . . . love. We juxtapose Jesus with our drive to be impressive and successful in our careers (which, as you might guess, is an impulse that tends to run wild in and around an ambition and achievement mecca like Yale). We juxtapose Jesus with our obsession to get the most out of life in the experiential, consumerist sense.

Matt tells me that the drive to maximize accomplishments and experiences is especially striking among the generally brilliant and motivated undergraduates who have managed to get into Yale. He knows because he was one of them, and because he teaches an unusual undergraduate course called "A Life Worth Living" (which I sat in on once). A generally nonreligious population, these students use acronyms like YOLO ("you only live once") and FOMO ("fear of missing out") to describe their compulsion to do a lot with their time and their lives. They have the intelligence and talent and drive to accomplish virtually anything. But as William

Deresiewicz observes in his book *Excellent Sheep*—the title describes the Yale undergraduates he once taught—they often have a hard time evaluating what is *worth* accomplishing.

Those of us at WTF? are older than undergraduate age—some of us significantly so—but it can hardly be said that the years have made us all enlightened in these respects. On our worst days, seculars can feel not only as though we lack a clear way to go when we reach the big forks in the road, but that we lack even the basic framework for conducting a coherent decision-making process. Hubert Dreyfus and Sean Dorrance Kelly capture this experience well in their book *All Things Shining*. The pair write, "It is not just that we know the course of right action and fail to pursue it; we often seem not to have any sense of what the standards of living a good life are in the first place. Or said another way, we seem to have no ground for choosing one course of action over any other."[2]

Although Jesus makes frequent appearances in our WTF? discussions, we don't all have the same ideas about him. He matters more to some of us than to others. But there does seem to be consensus around this notion:

Doing things as Jesus would have us do them is contrary to business as usual. And as that would imply, it's hard. One reason it's hard is that Jesus didn't dictate a precise and comprehensive manual for living. He told stories and gave examples, some of them rather cryptic and open to different interpretations. Dreyfus and Kelly write: "Jesus, as described in the gospels, does not provide a worked-out view of how to live. . . . But he shows luminously the new way of life."[3]

Not only is following Jesus hard in the difficult-to-figure-out sense, but it's hard in the sense that there is often a great deal of exertion involved, and a great deal of change that must be made. One of my Christian writer friends back in Portland had to call off his yearlong project to live just like Jesus and document the experience after he was diagnosed with epilepsy. "Not that following Jesus gave me seizures," he wrote in a message to his mailing list, "but all the added pressure was wreaking havoc on my health."

What an advertisement: Following Jesus might be bad for your health!

Don't say I didn't warn you.

More Than a Nice Idea

Because Jesus-following is so hard, if I am left to my own devices, with no structure, no consistent practices, no community of accountability, no one to remind me of my commitment or let me know when I am failing to walk the talk, I am likely to bend my understanding of Jesus, my putative "leader," into the most shallow, convenient, and distorted shapes. Truly, I have heard people (including the guy in my head) imagine Jesus in the most dubious ways: Jesus as a hard-charging man's man who would probably be an athlete were he around today, and who would take you out at second base, clean but hard, to break up the double play. Jesus as your party friend, totally chill, down with whatever, and always glad to smoke a bowl with you. Jesus as the kind of ardent liberal activist you run into at a political meeting, fired up about organizing workers, mobilizing voters, and influencing legislation—but not concerned about what's happening in your personal life.

Following Jesus as a nonreligious person can end up being as thin and light as a piece of paper, I realize. (It can for church people, too—a story for a different time.) Nice idea, we might say. How quaint. *Sure, I'm in favor of Jesus and some of these teachings he's famous for. What's not to like? Being nice to other people is good. Being less selfish—always something to strive for! Nice to realize that these already describe me, more or less. I mean, no one can realistically expect me to drop everything I'm doing and everything I own and follow Jesus like the disciples, right? Sure. I'm down with Jesus!*

To be clear, inch-deep engagement is preferable to wholesale rejection of the Jesus way—which is, when you think about it, difficult to imagine anyone articulating. Rarely if ever have I heard someone say, *No, Jesus was totally wrong! Being kind and compassionate is for losers! The point of life is to do and get as much as we can!* Okay, okay, so maybe we *have* observed a lot of people rejecting Jesus along these lines, albeit with their actions rather than their words. This rejection by action is, in fact, the very reason why the idealist in me is so drawn to Jesus, and why I make the claim that this ethic, this inspiration, could be such a difference maker in our lives and society today.

But, no, inch-deep is not what I'm talking about, even though it's a starting point and better than no depth at all. I'm talking about a kind of Jesus following that is more than a nice idea. I'm talking about a kind of Jesus following where there's really nothing in it for us by the usual formulas and ways of doing life, and where we are ready to screw ourselves and our own self-interest for the sake of doing the principled, idealistic thing, whether the other human being involved in the "transaction" is our friend or our colleague or our spouse or our parent or our child or the person who cleans the toilets in the building where we work or someone halfway around the world who is being trafficked or poisoned or the asshole on Facebook who pisses us off on a daily basis.

I am talking about getting on board with a conception of Jesus that doesn't justify who I am now and vindicate how I am living now but, rather, changes that "who" and that "how."

And for this, I insist, someone needs structure, practices, inputs, and perhaps most important, some kind of community or network.

If you're with me on that, let's go to our trusty information-finding friend Google now and look for a secular Jesus followers group in our community. Hmmm. The results are disappointing, aren't they? Some of the results I'm finding aren't *too* far off the mark. There's a secular Bible study meetup in Minneapolis, I see. I'm encouraged to find that there is also a website called Atheists for Jesus. But there doesn't seem to be any group out there for "secular Jesus followers." Anywhere.

No worries. We can be resourceful. We can be creative. We can be entrepreneurial. There are lots of ways to put flesh on these Jesus-following bones. There are books about Jesus—an enormous amount of them, some even written for nonreligious readers. There are churches, which for many less secular readers may be the best places for developing a Jesus-shaped life. There are plenty of discussion groups and meetups out there exploring life's big questions, and even though they are not about a secular Jesus way of life per se, they are certainly good contexts in which to develop and apply this idea, and to contribute to others who are likewise trying to deepen their lives. There are groups that do not yet exist but that indeed could exist—if you and your friends started them. There are conversations happening online that you can plug into. (I'm happy to discuss the idea with you, too, and fill you in on opportunities I know about. You can find my contact information at tomkrattenmaker.com and send me an e-mail. And by all means, let's continue the conversation on Twitter. #SecularJesus.)

But, please, if following Jesus is resonating with you and it's something you feel compelled to do, don't rely solely on your own wits and resources. You will not get far.

The Crowd Standing Apart from the Crowd

Really, the ethic that compels us all to be originals, to all be pioneers, to all stand out from the crowd is one of the absurdities of our time. As the late David Foster Wallace put it in a letter to an aspiring young writer: "There is this huge crowd of young people out here assembled and held together as a crowd solely by our fear of being crowd-swallowed. It is a paradox and a desperate plight."[4]

I'm sure Wallace was right about this dynamic having an especially strong hold on younger adults—it certainly did on me when I was in my twenties—but I suspect that if we start examining the crowd outside the crowd we will find a lot of not-so-young people, too.

It might seem equally absurd to imagine rejoining a crowd that has been emptied out and does not now exist.

But I do think that now is a time when more of us would do well to consider *following*—following someone or something, or maybe a well-considered assemblage of someone's and something's, and resist the lure of thinking we must always and only start from scratch in forming our worldview and governing body of ethics.

More, it's probably time we put the lie to the notion that all of us "independents" are so free from shepherds. As our WTF? discussion group explored at one memorable session, we might not be conscious of the grip that consumerism and ambition and fear and self-centeredness and other forces have on us, but they've got us, and we're following them, just the same. We are all following something, whether we know it or not. It is better to consciously choose who or what we are going to follow. It is better to choose, I say, and to choose well.

Me? I am choosing Jesus. Maybe it's partly because Jesus, of all the prophets and philosophers and "savior" figures in the pantheon, is the one with whom I am most familiar as a result of my growing up and living in a particular time and place. But conscious exploration has led to something deeper. The lure of this figure now has less to do with familiarity and more to do with the relationship I see him having to something about life that is so striking and disillusioning. It's that "something" that the head of Amnesty International has referred to as the "huge gap between the world we live in and the world we want."[5]

This Amnesty International leader, Salil Shetty, is referring to global scourges like poverty, inequality, and environmental degradation when he talks about the persistent gap between the world that is and the world we long for. The gap takes other forms, too. It's the gap we experience as individual human beings navigating the immediate world around us, where we have our ideas about what we want that world to be, what we think that world *should be*, but where we invariably find people misbehaving, people suffering, things getting screwed up, and everything seeming like a disillusioning mess. The gap between *should be* and *is* also appears inside each of us. It's the gap between our idea of how we ought to behave and treat other people, on the one hand, and what we actually do, on the other hand—the upsetting reality that we, too, can be instruments of disappointment and misery.

To put it another way, I realize that the reason I choose to follow Jesus is that his way is so antithetical, and such a powerful corrective, to aspects of life that are most disappointing and depressing.

No, even while acknowledging my capacity for self-deception, I perceive no God-size hole in my life. But as the foregoing suggests, there are holes, there are gaps, in the world we experience and the lives we live. These are not one-solution-fills-all holes; their size and shape vary and are ever-changing. Conventional religion can no longer fill the holes for increasing numbers of us in the Western world, present company included. But maybe because he has just the right amount of malleability, maybe because he did not dictate a rigid code or manual that was doomed to become outdated after a certain amount of time, Jesus seems to have transcended the context changes that have hamstrung codified religion as we know it. Jesus lives on with surprising vitality. Jesus remains a potent and compelling source, and force.

Here's to the people who manage Twitter. Let's give them a round of applause for posing, unwittingly, one of the most profound issues imaginable for our world and our time.

Indeed, who to follow?

I'm going with Jesus.

ACKNOWLEDGMENTS

The idea for this book was not my own. It was gifted by one of the most idealistic Jesus followers I know, a man who also happens to be a Christian. His name is Tony Kriz, or "Tony the Beat Poet," as he is called in a book beloved by many younger and middle-aged Christians, Donald Miller's *Blue Like Jazz*. Tony is not actually a poet, just so you know. But as Miller noticed, Tony sort of looks like one.

Having met as a result of my journalistic forays into evangelical culture, Tony and I often got together at Kell's pub in downtown Portland when I still lived in that great city. We would consume cigars and beer (nonalcoholic in my case; long story) while we discussed theology and writing and, as time went on, our lives. Tony came to know that I did not share his belief in God. He also learned that I thought and read a lot about the figure of Jesus, and that I had developed a deep appreciation for how the Jesus example, the Jesus way, could be transformative for the world—if only we could ever implement it, even partially.

During one memorable meetup, Tony and I discussed whether I should write a third book and, if I did, what it might be about. He broached an idea that, in retrospect, reminds me of the famously crazy and inspiring deed for which many know him, thanks to Miller's book. Tony was the one who instigated the legendary reverse confession booth at the heathen haven known as Reed College, where the Christians confessed to the oh-so-secular Reedies.

"Write a book," Tony told me, "imploring your fellow secular liberals to follow the way of Jesus."

I proceeded to do, more or less, what Tony said.

My deepest gratitude goes to Tony—not just for a book idea, but for being a good and kind friend and for showing me, perhaps better than anyone I've known, what it looks like to take Jesus-following to impressive and unrealistic heights and depths. Read his books *Neighbors and Wise Men* and *Aloof* if you want to know what I'm talking about.

In addition to Tony, I have many people to thank. One is my agent, Wes Yoder, whose vast experience, wisdom, and friendly enthusiasm propelled me and this project, and whose knack of knowing seemingly everyone in publishing led to our finding a great publisher.

Speaking of publishers, I send thanks as well to David Kopp at Convergent for his editorial guidance, his skilled hand, and his willingness to take a chance on this book and on me, a way-less-than-famous author.

I extend my appreciation to the people I work with at Yale Divinity School, including my boss, Dean Greg Sterling. YDS is a Christian school yet also a model of inclusiveness in the way it has tolerated and actually accepted my writing pursuits and secular ways. Especially deserving of credit in this regard is my friend Matthew Croasmun at the Center for Faith and Culture at YDS, who leads the center's "life worth living" project. If you didn't know better, you might expect that Matt's evangelical convictions would motivate him to oppose my book and secular engagement with Jesus. He has done the opposite and has served as a valuable source of support and insight.

I thank the many teachers and writers and editors and friends and coconspirators, in Portland and New Haven and around the country, who enlightened me on so many things and who furthered my development as a writer and human being.

And finally, I thank my wife, Carolyn Gretton, for her knowledge about and insights on many of the issues I discuss in this book. I have learned a lot from her. More important, I've received untold amounts of love, patience, and support.

NOTES

INTRODUCTION

1. The Barna Group, "Five Trends Among the Unchurched," October 9, 2014, https://www.barna.org/barna-update/culture/685-five-trends-among-the-unchurched#.VuviuKT2Y5s.
2. Shigehiro Oishi and Ed Diener, "Residents of Poor Nations Have a Greater Sense of Meaning in Life Than Residents of Wealthy Nations," *Psychological Science* 25, no. 2 (2014), pp. 422–430.
3. "The Equation of Change," *On Being with Krista Tippett*, March 13, 2014, http://www.onbeing.org/program/brian-mclaren-the-equation-of-change/6175.
4. Mark Sandlin, "I Want My Religion Back—You Can Keep the Ugly Baggage," Patheos, July 27, 2014, http://www.patheos.com/blogs/thegodarticle/2014/07/i-want-my-religion-back-you-can-keep-the-ugly-baggage/.

CHAPTER 1

1. Christopher Ingraham, "Anti-Muslim Hate Crimes Are Still Five Times More Common Today Than Before 9/11," *Washington Post*, February 11, 2015, https://www.washingtonpost.com/news/wonk/wp/2015/02/11/anti-muslim-hate-crimes-are-still-five-times-more-common-today-than-before-911/.
2. Robert D. Putnam and David E. Campbell, *American Grace: How Religion Divides and Unites Us* (Simon & Schuster, 2010), p. 527.

3. "Protesters Berate Muhammad During Anti-Islam Protest at Phoenix Mosque," *The Guardian*, May 30, 2015, http://www.theguardian.com/us-news/2015/may/30/protestors-berate-prophet-muhammad-at-anti-islam-protest-at-phoenix-mosque.
4. Willie Jennings, *The Christian Imagination, Theology and the Origins of Race* (Yale University Press, 2011), p. 287.
5. Charles P. Pierce, "I Hate Centrism," Esquire.com, October 16, 2013, http://www.esquire.com/news-politics/politics/a19653/response-to-new-american-center-101613/.

CHAPTER 2

1. Traci Watson, "7,000-year-old massacre shows signs of torture, mutilation," *USA Today*, August 18, 2015, http://www.usatoday.com/story/news/2015/08/17/massacre-bloodshed-7000-years-germany/31869013/.
2. "We Can't Bomb Our Way to Peace," *USA Today*, June 11, 2015, http://www.usatoday.com/story/opinion/2015/06/11/iraq-win-without-war-editorials-debates/71085642/.
3. Alejandro Azuero-Quijano, "Gaza's Tunnel Paradox," Al Jazeera America, August 14, 2014, http://america.aljazeera.com/opinions/2014/8/gaza-tunnel-siegeisraelidfblockade.html.
4. "Struggle for Equality: Quotes from Martin Luther King Jr.," Scholastic.com, http://www.scholastic.com/teachers/article/struggle-equality-quotes-martin-luther-king-jr.
5. Philip Kitcher, *Life After Faith: The Case for Secular Humanism* (Yale University Press, 2014), Kindle edition location 603.
6. Walter Wink, *The Powers That Be: Theology for a New Millennium* (Doubleday, 1999), Kindle edition location 1266; this portion of the book can also be accessed online at http://www.cpt.org/files/BN%20-%20Jesus'%20Third%20Way.pdf.
7. Walter Wink, *The Powers That Be: Theology for a New Millennium*, Kindle edition location 1329.
8. Ibid., location 1285.
9. "The Christian Ideal," The American Chesterton Society, http://www.chesterton.org/the-christian-ideal/.

CHAPTER 3

1. Nancy Jo Sales, "Tinder and the Dawn of the 'Dating Apocalypse,'" *Vanity Fair*, September 2015, http://www.vanityfair.com/culture/2015/08/tinder-hook-up-culture-end-of-dating.

2. Uki Goni, "Argentine Women Call Out Machismo," *New York Times*, June 15, 2015, http://www.nytimes.com/2015/06/16/opinion/argentine-women-call-out-machismo.html.
3. Uki Goni, "Argentine Women Call Out Machismo," *New York Times*, June 15, 2015.
4. This line is often attributed to the novelist Margaret Atwood. While Atwood is on the record as making this general point, something closer to the exact wording is found in the Gavin de Becker book *The Gift of Fear* (Bantam Doubleday Dell, 1998), p. 77.
5. Nick Anderson, Susan Svrluga, and Scott Clement, "Survey: More Than 1 in 5 Female Undergrads at Top Schools Suffer Sexual Attacks," *Washington Post*, September 21, 2015, https://www.washingtonpost.com/local/education/survey-more-than-1-in-5-female-undergrads-at-top-schools-suffer-sexual-attacks/2015/09/19/c6c80be2-5e29-11e5-b38e-06883aacba64_story.html.
6. It should be acknowledged that the patterns of abuse and exploitation described in this chapter take place, too, in the trans and LGBT communities. See, for example, Maya Shwayder, "A Same-Sex Domestic Violence Epidemic Is Silent," *The Atlantic*, November 5, 2013, http://www.theatlantic.com/health/archive/2013/11/a-same-sex-domestic-violence-epidemic-is-silent/281131/.
7. Some conservatives and/or traditionalists will no doubt contest this point, contending that while it is technically true that Jesus did not talk about homosexuality, his condemnation of it is implicit in what he says about relationships between men and women. For an example of this argument and a pathway to related sources, see: "If homosexuality is a sin, why didn't Jesus ever mention it?" Gotquestions.org, http://www.gotquestions.org/Jesus-homosexuality.html.
8. For a good overview of the effect of divorce on children, see "An Overview of the Psychological Literature on the Effects of Divorce on Children," a report by the American Psychological Association, May 2004, http://www.apa.org/about/gr/issues/cyf/divorce.aspx.
9. John Sides, "Americans Have Become More Opposed to Adultery. Why?" *The Monkey Cage*, July 27, 2011, themonkeycage.org/2011/07/americans-have-become-more-opposed-to-adultery-why/.
10. Amy R. Buckley, "Yoga Pants and What the Bible Really Says About Modesty," *Relevant*, May 21, 2015, http://www.relevantmagazine.com/life/yoga-pants-and-what-Bible-really-says-about-modesty.
11. Credit for this insight on the story is owed to Matthew Croasmun and his booklet *Questions Jesus Asks*, published by Croasmun's church, Elm City Vineyard, 2013; see p. 14.

12. Harvey Cox, *How to Read the Bible* (HarperOne, 2015), p. 139.
13. "Rashida Jones' Documentary Shows How Porn Companies Lure Teenage Girls," "*FOX411*," May 29, 2015, http://www.foxnews.com/entertainment/2015/05/29/rashida-jones-new-doc-investigates-how-porn-companies-are-luring-teenage-girls/.
14. Amanda Hess, "How Many Women Are Not Admitting to Pew That They Watch Porn?" *Slate*, October 11, 2013, http://www.slate.com/blogs/xx_factor/2013/10/11/pew_online_viewing_study_percentage_of_women_who_watch_online_porn_is_growing.html.
15. Naomi Wolf, "The Porn Myth," *New York*, October 20, 2003, http://nymag.com/nymetro/news/trends/n_9437/.
16. See, for example: Tyler Kingkade, "Texas Tech Frat Loses Charter Following 'No Means Yes, Yes Means Anal' Display," Huffington Post, October 8, 2014, http://www.huffingtonpost.com/2014/10/08/texas-tech-frat-no-means-yes_n_5953302.html. This chant has been heard as well at Yale University.
17. For some readers, abortion will come to mind as the most obvious and egregious example. For my own nuanced treatment of the abortion issue, see chapter 8, "Pro-Life . . . Seriously," of my book *The Evangelicals You Don't Know* (Rowman & Littlefield, 2013).
18. See, for instance, "Strip Clubs: Where Prostitution and Trafficking Happen" (Prostitution Research & Education, December 2013), http://prostitutionresearch.com/pre_blog/2013/10/07/strip-clubs-where-prostitution-and-trafficking-happen/.
19. Ross Douthat, "The Caligulan Thrill," *New York Times*, February 14, 2015, http://www.nytimes.com/2015/02/15/opinion/sunday/ross-douthat-the-caligulan-thrill.html.

CHAPTER 4

1. Taylor Clark, "It's Not the Job Market: The three real reasons why Americans are more anxious than ever before," *Slate*, January 31, 2011, http://www.slate.com/articles/arts/culturebox/2011/01/its_not_the_job_market.html.
2. Taylor Clark, "It's Not the Job Market: The three real reasons why Americans are more anxious than ever before," *Slate*, January 31, 2011.
3. Amy Simpson, *Anxious: Choosing Faith in a World of Worry* (InterVarsity Press, 2014), p. 23.
4. Matt Croasmun, *Questions Jesus Asks* (Elm City Vineyard, 2013), p. 22.

5. "Choosing Faith in a World of Worry: Q and A with Amy Simpson," published at the website Ink: A Creative Collection, October 25, 2014, http://www.inkcreative.org/choosing-faith-in-a-world-of-worry-a-qa-with-amy-simpson/.
6. To clarify, I am speaking here not about all aspects of Jesus's prescription for worry and anxiety, e.g,, turning to God, but about his diagnosis of its prevalence and effects and his teachings about the need to avoid or at least minimize its ravages. Some readers will note, too, instances in the gospels where Jesus flashes anger or departs in other ways from the equanimity I am speaking of here. So be it. I am confident my assertion is accurate in the aggregate.

CHAPTER 5

1. Miroslav Volf and Ryan McAnnally-Linz, "What Makes Life Worth Living? Take a Moment to Ask," *The World Post*, August 25, 2014, http://www.huffingtonpost.com/miroslav-volf/what-makes-life-worth-living_b_5710227.html.
2. David Brooks, "The Act of Rigorous Forgiving," *New York Times*, February 10, 2015, http://www.nytimes.com/2015/02/10/opinion/david-brooks-the-act-of-rigorous-forgiving.html.
3. David Brooks, "The Ambition Explosion," *New York Times*, November 27, 2014, http://www.nytimes.com/2014/11/28/opinion/david-brooks-the-ambition-explosion.html.
4. Sara Miles, "Give Us Bread," *Reflections*, Fall 2014, http://reflections.yale.edu/article/risk-our-food-our-water-ourselves/give-us-bread.
5. Beth Stebner, "Workplace Morale Heads Down: 70% of Americans Negative About Their Jobs, Gallup Study Shows," *New York Daily News*, June 24, 2013, http://www.nydailynews.com/news/national/70-u-s-workers-hate-job-poll-article-1.1381297.
6. James K. A. Smith, *How (Not) to Be Secular: Reading Charles Taylor* (Wm. B. Eerdmans, 2014), p. 129.
7. Charles Taylor, *A Secular Age* (Harvard University Press, 2007), p. 309.

CHAPTER 6

1. Alain de Botton, *Religion for Atheists* (Random House, 2012), p. 27.
2. Vishaan Chakrabarti, "America's Urban Future," *New York Times*, April 16, 2014, http://www.nytimes.com/2014/04/17/opinion/americas-urban-future.html?_r=0.

3. "Global Health Observatory Data," World Health Organization, http://www.who.int/gho/urban_health/situation_trends/urban_population_growth_text/en/.

4. Philip Kitcher, *Life After Faith: The Case of Secular Humanism* (Yale University Press, 2014), location 653.

5. Jerilyn Veldof and Corey Bonnema, "Minnesota Nice? It's Like Ice," *Minneapolis–St. Paul Star Tribune,* June 11, 2014, http://m.startribune.com/?id=266823811.

6. Jerilyn Veldof and Corey Bonnema, "Minnesota Nice? It's Like Ice," *Minneapolis–St. Paul Star Tribune,* June 11, 2014.

7. de Botton, *Religion for Atheists,* p. 29.

8. Alfred Lubrano, "Among the 10 Largest Cities, Philly Has Highest Deep-Poverty Rate," *Philadelphia Inquirer,* October 1, 2015, http://articles.philly.com/2015-10-01/news/67015543_1_poverty-rate-deep-poverty-philadelphians.

9. Alfred Lubrano, "Report: Pa. area among hungriest: The First Congressional District, including parts of Phila. and Chester, is ranked 2d-worst in U.S.," *Philadelphia Inquirer,* January 26, 2010, http://articles.philly.com/2010-01-26/news/25210328_1_hardship-food-research-hunger.

CHAPTER 7

1. Joseph Shapiro, "Unpaid Court Fees Land the Poor in Twenty-first Century Debtors' Prisons," National Public Radio, May 20, 2014, http://www.kplu.org/post/unpaid-court-fees-land-poor-21st-century-debtors-prisons.

2. Roy Walmsley, "World Prison Population List (tenth edition)" (International Centre for Prison Studies, November 21, 2013), http://www.prisonstudies.org/sites/default/files/resources/downloads/wppl_10.pdf.

3. Stav Ziv, "Report: America's Prison Population Is Growing Again," Newsweek.com, December 22, 2014, http://www.newsweek.com/americas-correctional-system-numbers-293583.

4. Kathleen Miles, "Just How Much the War on Drugs Impacts Our Overcrowded Prisons, in One Chart," Huffington Post, April 3, 2014, http://www.huffingtonpost.com/2014/03/10/war-on-drugs-prisons-infographic_n_4914884.html.

5. Karen Dolan with Jodi L. Car, "The Poor Get Prison: The Alarming Spread of the Criminalization of Poverty" (Institute for Policy Studies,

March 2015), http://www.ips-dc.org/wp-content/uploads/2015/03/IPS-The-Poor-Get-Prison-Final.pdf.

6. "Report of the Sentencing Project to the United Nations Human Rights Committee," The Sentencing Project, August 2013, http://sentencingproject.org/doc/publications/rd_ICCPR%20Race%20and%20Justice%20Shadow%20Report.pdf. Note: Some critics argue that the figure is exaggerated; even so, it seems incontestable that dramatically larger percentages of African-American males are imprisoned than white.
7. Abby Haglage, "New School Study Shows Black Kids Get Cops, White Kids Get Docs," *The Daily Beast*, July 30, 2015, http://www.thedailybeast.com/articles/2015/07/30/new-school-study-shows-black-kids-get-cops-white-kids-get-docs.html.
8. Shapiro, "Unpaid Court Fees."
9. Aimee Picchi, "The High Price of Incarceration in America," CBSNews.com, May 8, 2014, http://www.cbsnews.com/news/the-high-price-of-americas-incarceration-80-billion.
10. Michael Mitchell and Michael Leachman, "Changing Priorities: State Criminal Justice Reforms and Investments in Education" (Center on Budget and Policy Priorities, October 28, 2014), http://www.cbpp.org//sites/default/files/atoms/files/10-28-14sfp.pdf.
11. Rebecca Klein, "States Are Prioritizing Prisons over Education, Budgets Show," Huffington Post, October 30, 2014, http://www.huffingtonpost.com/2014/10/30/state-spending-prison-and-education_n_6072318.html.
12. Katherine Reynolds Lewis, "What If Everything You Knew About Disciplining Kids Was Wrong?" *Mother Jones*, July/August 2015, http://www.motherjones.com/authors/katherine-reynolds-lewis.
13. Erik Eckholm, "Out of Prison, and Staying Out, After Third Strike in California," *New York Times*, February 26, 2015, http://www.nytimes.com/2015/02/27/us/california-convicts-are-out-of-prison-after-third-strike-and-staying-out.html.
14. Kimberly Grenade, "Orange is the New Black and the Reality of Recidivism," activate, a blog published by Met Council on Housing, June 17, 2014, http://www.everythinghousing.org/2014/07/orange-is-new-black-and-reality-of.html.
15. Audrey Bazos and Jessica Hausman, "Correctional Education as a Crime Control Program" (UCLA School of Public Policy and Social Research, Department of Policy Studies, March 2004), http://www.ceanational.org/PDFs/ed-as-crime-control.pdf.

16. Ellis Cose, "Reform Criminal Justice Now," *USA Today*, August 3, 2015, http://www.usatoday.com/story/opinion/2015/08/02/criminal-justice-reform-needed-society-movement-column/31020317/.

17. Chase Madar, "Everyone Is a Criminal: On the Over-policing of America," *The Nation*, December 9, 2013, http://www.thenation.com/article/everyone-criminal-over-policing-america. See also Glenn Greenwald, "Denny Hastert Is Contemptible, but His Indictment Exemplifies America's Over-Criminalization Pathology," *The Intercept*, May 29, 2015, https://firstlook.org/theintercept/2015/05/29/denny-hastert-highly-unsympathetic-face-americas-criminalization-pathology.

18. Alex Kozinski and Misha Tseytlin, "You're (Probably) a Federal Criminal," in *In the Name of Justice: Leading Experts Reexamine the Classic Article "The Aims of the Criminal Law,"* ed. Timothy Lynch (Cato Institute, 2009), p. 44, https://books.google.com.br/books?id=Tu5RB6YHf10C&pg=PA43&dq=probably+a+federal&hl=en&sa=X&ei=KWVoVZOQAYr6sAW3nYPQDA&ved=0CB0Q6AEwAA#v=onepage&q=probably%20a%20federal&f=false.

CHAPTER 8

1. Rich Exner, "Witness Accounts in Tamir Rice Investigation Paint Vivid Picture of Events," *Cleveland Plain Dealer*, June 13, 2015, http://www.cleveland.com/metro/index.ssf/2015/06/witness_accounts_in_tamir_rice.html.

2. Danielle Kurtzleben, "The Median Wealth for Whites in the U.S. Is Nearly $142,000. For Blacks, It's $11,000," *Vox*, December 13, 2014, http://www.vox.com/2014/12/13/7383033/the-median-wealth-for-whites-in-the-us-is-nearly-142000-for-blacks.

3. Glenn L. Starks and F. Erik Brooks, *African Americans at Risk: Issues in Education, Health, Community, and Justice* (Greenwood, ABC-CLIO, 2015) p. 271.

4. Josh Mitchell, "About Half of Kids with Single Moms Live in Poverty," *Wall Street Journal*, November 25, 2013, http://blogs.wsj.com/economics/2013/11/25/about-half-of-kids-with-single-moms-live-in-poverty.

5. Ta-Nehisi Coates, "The Black Family in the Age of Mass Incarceration," *Atlantic*, October 2015, http://www.theatlantic.com/magazine/archive/2015/10/the-black-family-in-the-age-of-mass-incarceration/403246/#Chapter%20III.

6. Howard Bryant, "By This Measure, Michael Jordan Can't Touch LeBron James," ABCNews website, September 2, 2015, http://

abcnews.go.com/Sports/measure-michael-jordan-touch-lebron-james/story?id=33480429.

7. For instance, a University of Illinois study documents that people are quicker to shoot black targets with guns than white targets. See "Study: Shooters Quicker to Pull Trigger if Target Is Black," CBS St. Louis, August 31, 2015, http://stlouis.cbslocal.com/2015/08/31/study-shooters-quicker-to-pull-trigger-if-target-is-black/.
8. Lisa Sharon Harper, "How Religion Became a Destructive—and Redemptive—Force for 'Black Lives Matter,'" *Washington Post*, April 9, 2015, http://www.washingtonpost.com/news/acts-of-faith/wp/2015/04/09/how-religion-became-a-destructive-and-redemptive-force-for-black-lives-matter/?tid=sm_tw.
9. For a thorough and fascinating exploration of the relationship between Christianity and slavery, see Albert J. Raboteau, *Slave Religion: The "Invisible Institution" in the Antebellum South*, 25th anniversary ed. (Oxford University Press, 2004).
10. "A Growing Divide on Race," *New York Times*/CBS News Poll, July 23, 2015, http://www.nytimes.com/interactive/2015/07/23/us/race-relations-in-america-poll.html.

CHAPTER 9

1. Stephen L. Carter, *God's Name in Vain: The Wrongs and Rights of Religion in Politics* (Basic Books, 2001), p. 27.
2. History shows that Hamer's efforts in 1964 yielded something well short of the "beginning of the new kingdom." In fact, no one from her delegation was seated. A larger victory was coming, however. In 1968, the party adopted a clause demanding equality of representation in each of the state's delegations, and members of the Democratic Freedom Party indeed were seated. In 1972, Hamer was elected a national party delegate. For more, see: Steven Lemongello, "Black Mississippians create legacy," *Press of Atlantic City*, August 24, 2014, http://www.pressofatlanticcity.com/communities/atlantic-city_pleasantville_brigantine/black-mississippians-create-legacy/article_9811ec34-2bdd-11e4-92f4-0019bb2963f4.html.
3. Tom Krattenmaker, "A Discussion with Stephen L. Carter," September 12, 2011, http://tomkrattenmaker.com/?p=485.
4. Kirsten Powers, "Give the 'Bigot' Bomb a Rest," *USA Today*, May 26, 2015, http://www.usatoday.com/story/opinion/2015/05/26/christian-marriage-davage-rhetoric-column/27960079/.
5. Jonathan Haidt, "Defusing Political Conflicts: A Q&A with Jonathan Haidt About How Liberals and Conservatives Can Band

Together," *TEDBlog,* January 7, 2013, http://blog.ted.com/defusing-political-conflicts-a-qa-with-jonathan-haidt-about-how-liberals-and-conservatives-can-band-together/.

6. Readers should not take this comment on the success of pro football as my endorsement of the enterprise or an indication that I am a fan. For reasons I have articulated in *USA Today,* I have stopped watching the NFL. See: Tom Krattenmaker, "Is It Immoral to Watch the Super Bowl?" *USA Today,* February 1, 2016, http://www.usatoday.com/story/opinion/2016/02/01/super-bowl-football-brain-damage-immoral-watch-column/79654086/.

CHAPTER 10

1. John Duncan and William Angus Knight, *Colloquia Peripatetica* (Edinburgh: Edmonston, Douglas, 1870), p. 109, https://books.google.com/books?id=LUcMAAAAIAAJ&pg=PR7&lpg=PR7&dq=colloquia+peripatetica+page+109&source=bl&ots=W5qRYIeXvx&sig=K-LKg53sHb2obtV9xsuk7kKoex4&hl=en&sa=X&ved=0ahUKEwin6_qm5ZPLAhUJaT4KHSqbA1YQ6AEIKDAD#v=onepage&q=colloquia%20peripatetica%20page%20109&f=false.
2. Hubert Dreyfus and Sean Dorrance Kelly, *All Things Shining: Reading the Western Classics to Find Meaning in a Secular Age* (Free Press, 2011), Kindle edition location 1677.
3. Alain de Botton, "Easter for Atheists," The Philosophers' Mail, http://thephilosophersmail.com/utopia/easter-for-atheists.
4. Brandon Ambrosino, "Jesus' Radical Politics," *Boston Globe,* April 1, 2015, https://www.bostonglobe.com/opinion/2015/04/01/jesus-radical-politics/txdjkQSMn3BWPBgciEbgZP/story.html#.
5. Michael M. Grynbaum, "De Blasio, Inspired by Francis, Describes an Evolving Relationship With Faith," *New York Times,* July 22, 2015, http://www.nytimes.com/2015/07/23/nyregion/de-blasio-inspired-by-francis-describes-an-evolving-relationship-with-faith.html.

EPILOGUE

1. Chris Stedman, *Faitheist: How an Atheist Found Common Ground with the Religious* (Beacon Press, 2013).
2. Hubert Dreyfus and Sean Dorrance Kelly, *All Things Shining: Reading the Western Classics to Find Meaning in a Secular Age* (Free Press, 2011), Kindle edition location 348.
3. Ibid., location 1723.

4. Molly Beauchemin, "I Transcribed This David Foster Wallace Letter from a Picture," April 14, 2014, http://mollybeauchemin.tumblr.com/post/82657097433/i-transcribed-this-david-foster-wallace-letter.
5. Ellen Wulfhorst, "Leaders call for 'less conversation, more action' after adopting U.N. global goals," September 25, 2015, http://www.reuters.com/article/2015/09/26/us-development-goals-adoption-idUSKCN0RP2FL20150926.